Homeowner's Guide to Swimming Pools

Ronald Derven and Carol Nichols

Ideals Publishing Corp.
Milwaukee, Wisconsin

Table of Contents

ISBN 0-8249-6116-1

Copyright © 1982 by Ideals Publishing Corporation

All rights reserved. This book or parts thereof, may not be reproduced in any form without permission of the copyright owners. Printed and bound in the United States of America. Published simultaneously in Canada.

Published by Ideals Publishing Corporation
11315 Watertown Plank Road
Milwaukee, Wisconsin 53226

Editor, David Schansberg

Cover photo courtesy of Hedrich-Blessing

SUCCESSFUL
HOME IMPROVEMENT SERIES

Bathroom Planning and Remodeling
Kitchen Planning and Remodeling
Space Saving Shelves and Built-ins
Finishing Off Additional Rooms
Finding and Fixing the Older Home
Money Saving Home Repair Guide
Homeowner's Guide to Tools
Homeowner's Guide to Electrical Wiring
Homeowner's Guide to Plumbing
Homeowner's Guide to Roofing and Siding
Homeowner's Guide to Fireplaces
Home Plans for the '80s
Planning and Building Home Additions
Homeowner's Guide to Concrete and Masonry
Homeowner's Guide to Landscaping
Homeowner's Guide to Swimming Pools
Homeowner's Guide to Fastening Anything
Planning and Building Vacation Homes
Homeowner's Guide to Floors and Staircases
Home Appliance Repair Guide
Homeowner's Guide to Wood Refinishing
Children's Rooms and Play Areas
Wallcoverings: Paneling, Painting, and Papering
Money Saving Natural Energy Systems
How to Build Your Own Home

Preliminary Planning and Considerations

While you may have given some thought to having a swimming pool in your own backyard or home, you probably always figured you would need a great deal of money to make your dream a reality. But, swimming pools are no longer just for the rich. Because of new materials and manufacturing techniques, a family can purchase a relatively inexpensive pool. Today, it is simply a question of wanting one. Costs generally range between $1,000 and $20,000.

For $1,000 or slightly less, a small above-ground pool about 15 feet in diameter, with a filtration system, can be purchased and easily erected by the homeowner. An above-ground pool can cost several thousand dollars if you are talking about a sizeable pool with a variety of features, such as a diving board and a large deck.

Since Americans spend more time swimming than at any other outdoor sport it should come as no sur-

prise that an increasing number of families build or buy a swimming pool each year. Even though neighborhood pools are within driving distance, there are reasons why the lure of private recreation makes a pool seem like a sound investment.

We are more concerned today with physical fitness and health than ever before, and doctors tell us that swimming is one of the ideal ways to keep fit. Swimming is the best overall aerobic exercise. It exercises all the muscles, especially those of the heart and lungs. It also offers recreational togetherness for the entire family.

Getting to a nearby place to swim can cost a great deal in terms of money and aggravation, and in the end it can mean disappointment. Climbing onto the hot vinyl upholstery to go to a pool or dripping onto the seat on the way back, paying for gasoline and entrance fees, and fighting overcrowded beaches, highways, and pools do not encourage families who want to take the time and effort to go to a public pool or beach. Other private bathing facilities such as country clubs and swim clubs may involve traffic problems and high yearly costs. If a would-be pool owner also adds in what he spends on summer camps and expensive family vacations, a backyard pool begins to look better for his pocketbook in the long run.

The key phrase is "in the long run" when you are talking about in-ground pools as an investment. The pool obviously adds to the resale value of your home. Real estate prices have traditionally kept up with the rate of inflation; so if you install one and prices continue to climb, the value of your pool may increase every year. If and when you sell your home, the initial investment of an added swimming pool may be returned to you in full. A good rule of thumb is that the investment should be about 20 percent or less of your home value. On the other hand if you add a $20,000 pool to a house which is valued at $70,000, you will have a very fine pool, but you should plan to stay in your home for a long time or take a loss at resale. Real estate agents say that in expensive neighborhoods the addition of a pool can usually return far more at resale than the owner's original investment. This, of course, also depends on the condition of the housing market at resale and how long an owner can hold out to get the price he or she is demanding.

Swimming pools are an excellent investment for you and the cost of your pool can be returned in full at resale. To recapture most or all of your cost, keep the pool at 20 percent or less the value of your home. The in-ground vinyl-lined pool above fits in well with the home. Photo courtesy of National Swimming Pool Institute

Financing, Expenses, and Deductions

Today's cost of an average-sized in-ground pool, according to the National Spa and Pool Institute (NSPI), will run about $9,000 if you live in the Northeast, Midwest, Northwest, California, Hawaii, and the Southwest; it costs slightly less in the South and more in the Rocky Mountain states. There are many local variations that influence cost. In highly competitive urban areas where many good pool dealers and builders can be found, you might be able to get a better price. In suburban and rural areas, there are usually fewer contractors and pool dealers, so your price quotations may be higher.

Because most lending institutions look upon in-ground pool additions as a home improvement, financing is usually handled by a bank. This, however, does not apply to the Federal Housing Administration (FHA). A typical home improvement loan can be obtained at the prevailing interest rate and paid back monthly over a specific number of years. Lower interest rates can be obtained through life-insurance loans, bank collateral loans, and passbook loans. If you belong to a credit union, you may be able to arrange an even lower cost loan. Try to avoid financing through consumer credit loans and refinancing your mortgage. The consumer finance organizations make loans easy to obtain, but they usually charge higher interest and life-insurance rates. Refinancing your mortgage may offer low interest rates, but you will be paying for the next 15 to 25 years on a larger amount of money, which could make the actual price of your swimming pool soar.

Traditionally, savings and loan associations usually charge less than commercial banks for home-improvement loans. Of course when money is tight, your local commercial bank may be the only source in town.

Financing may make it easier for the would-be pool owner to save money at the planning stage. You can plan and pay for the installation of such things as pool heaters or underwater lights rather than doing so in the future. Added-on features usually cost much more.

Included in your financial figures should be the actual cost of running and maintaining your pool—about $35-$75 per month for an in-ground pool without heating and about $25 to $35 for an above-ground pool. The many options, at varying prices, are discussed later in the book. Also, when penciling out what an in-ground pool will cost you, don't forget to add yearly taxes. Because an in-ground pool is considered a permanent improvement, called an accessory structure, the tax assessor will bill you anywhere from $50 to $200 a year on it. In most cases the tax rate is based on around one-half the cost of the pool. This tax is deductible on your federal income tax and so is the sales tax on a pool's installation. Again, if you finance your swimming pool, the interest paid on the loan is also fully deductible from federal and state income taxes.

The above-ground pool is not considered a permanent improvement. It is untaxed and is usually ineligible for financing through a home-improvement loan. In all cases, check with your bank or mortgage holder.

Some families who wish to decrease the expense of an in-ground pool or wish to make it a joint responsibility build a multifamily pool.

Cutting Through Red Tape

Unfortunately you may be able to afford a swimming pool and still not be able to build an in-ground pool in your backyard because of local building restrictions or site inadequacies. There are three items you must check as part of your basic prepool planning.

Building and Health Departments First check with your local building and health departments to determine whether or not a pool is allowed in your area. Most municipalities will allow pools, but there are various restrictions and covenants which you must follow. Some may be so costly or complex that it would not be worthwhile to build your pool.

This also means looking into building permit requirements for your accessory structures and decks. Local building and health departments will give you the necessary information on health standards, setback distances, pool fencing, and whether the pool site must be inspected during the building process. Permits are often issued on the basis of specific plans. If so,

Above-ground pools offer a lot of "swimmability" for the dollar invested. They are not considered a permanent improvement; therefore, they are not taxed. Photo courtesy of Coleco Industries, Inc.

Concrete and vinyl-liner in-ground pools are considered a home improvement by financial institutions and the tax man. Although these pools add to the resale value of your home, it will also add to your yearly tax burden. Photo courtesy of National Swimming Pool Institute

draw up all the details and submit them to the proper authorities. Also find out how many times and at what stages the building site requires inspection. Soil tests may be required to determine soil stability and prevent excessive slippage.

House Deed Review your house deed for building restrictions. Also look carefully for any easements on your lot for telephone and power line installations.

If you discover severe obstacles, you may wish to follow up and inquire about variances from local zoning boards. Special permits are granted under unusual circumstances, and you may well qualify; but you must ask. No one will volunteer the information.

This may sound like a good deal of legwork, but in most cases these steps can be accomplished in several hours. If you prefer, you can have your attorney do the work for you. But in all cases a would-be pool owner is responsible for making sure that the pool site has been cleared by the proper authorities before excavation begins. The contractor or the landscape architect will usually assume this has been done.

After you are positive you are within the regulations permitting you to build a swimming pool on your property, zero in on the last item.

Property Survey Go over the survey of your property to determine your property lines. Then place down markers. Do not assume you remember where they are. Be careful, because virtually every town or city ordinance has setback and side-yard requirements for accessory structures. In some towns it might be only 20 feet; in others it could be more.

After determining the setback requirements, draw them in your survey in pencil. Now answer the following questions:

- Does the remaining space allow for a pool? An average-sized pool runs from 15 by 30 feet to 20 by 40 feet. Smaller pools are available, but plan on

36 square feet per swimmer and 100 square feet of water per diver to see what your family's needs require. A 12 by 27-foot pool is usually considered the minimum practical size. Also figure about 3 or 4 feet of decking around the pool and storage space for a pump and filter.

- Is there access from the road to the pool site for heavy equipment? Make sure you have a 7 or 8-foot clear path which will accommodate the digging machinery and heavy trucks. Your pool costs will jump considerably if the excavation equipment cannot get through and the site must be dug by hand, or if the concrete truck cannot deliver to the exact spot and concrete has to be hand carried or pumped. If your favorite tree or shrubs are in that path, they must be transplanted or cut down.

- What is underground in that area, such as sewer or septic systems or utility lines? The depth of the pool is generally between 3 and 12 feet. A pool cannot be excavated if there are gas lines, buried telephone wires, sewer pipes, septic tanks, or water lines under the site. These are extremely costly and troublesome to move. The best solution if

they are in the way is to change your site. If this is not possible, you might look at various above-ground pools, which require little or no excavation.

If one or several of the above-mentioned obstructions are buried on the pool site and you still choose to build there, an excavator will watch out for them, but cannot guarantee that he will not hit them. It is your responsibility, and your risk, whether or not you tell the contractor they are there. Some contractors will move the lines and split the cost with the owner rather than chance hitting them. But find out beforehand. It is wise to resolve each major question before firmly committing yourself to building an in-ground swimming pool.

- Do you have more than one possible site for a swimming pool on your land?

Other questions you may have, such as selecting one of various pool sites on your land, shaded versus sunny areas, shrub and tree problems, attaining maximum privacy, drainage problems, or difficult land grading, can be discussed with the appropriate technician to your advantage.

Your property may not have as much space on which to place a pool as above. Before you get too deeply involved, check with your building department and health department to determine whether you can comply with setback and fencing requirements. Photo courtesy of Heldor Associates

Planning and Designing the Perfect Pool

Now that you have decided you definitely want a pool, how do you figure out which one is best suited to your life-style? First, look at your needs by sitting down with the family and discussing how and by whom the pool will be used. Then look at the cost, and you'll be able to plan the whole structure with a minimum of expense and aggravation.

Whatever your life-style, keep in mind that a swimming pool is more, much more, than simply an outdoor bathtub. It can and should become an outdoor recreation area. The pool needs a proper setting on your property and space for a terrace or deck. You should allow enough room around the pool for other entertainment and recreational activities so that they will not interfere with swimming.

Your Life-Style

First, discuss the following questions with your family. Will the pool be used primarily by small children now and in the future? Will the users want to practice diving? Will it be used to practice for competitive swimming and exercising, or just sunning and splashing? Will the pool be a private or a community project? How much does the family wish the pool to dominate its activities during the year? Will it be used for a lot of family socializing and entertaining? How much time and energy will the family be willing to devote to pool maintenance and still enjoy ownership?

Depending on your answers, you should be able to narrow down the type of swimming pool. First, figure out what would be your ideal in a swimming pool. Then make sensible choices to cut some of the costs of your dream pool.

If your pool is to be used mainly by small children, an above-ground pool might be a safer choice. You could plan for a more extensive in-ground pool later on. Or you can build an in-ground pool with a broad shallow end. When small children are involved, many families choose to locate the pool near the house because it is easier to keep an eye on it. There may be a constant stream of children running in and out of the house for snacks, towels, and bathroom facilities, but many prefer this inconvenience due to the safety factor. Small children quickly outgrow a pool designed for shallow-end activities or one with a special wading area. Include these areas only if you anticipate small children using the pool for many years.

Dimensions The depth of the pool can be dramatically affected by many aspects of your life-style, as already indicated by small children's activities. Assume that 3 feet is the minimum depth, but even nonswimmers prefer 3½ to 5 feet. Racing and turning require a 3½-foot depth, and divers must have at least 8½ feet of unobstructed depth. Competitive diving requires a minimum of 11 feet for a board 1 meter above the surface and a minimum of 15 feet of headroom.

Length and width should be considered along the same lines. The width of the pool should be at least 15 feet, and the distance from the deep-end wall to the 5-foot "break point" should be at least 22 feet. For serious swimming and exercising, it helps to conform your pool to U.S. Swimming competitive requirements. This would mean an even divisor of 75 feet, usually 25 or 37½ feet in length.

Multifamily Pools If a realistic evaluation of your living conditions includes your neighbors using the pool, you might sit down with them and find out if they would want to share your expenses on a joint or multifamily pool. Three, four, or more families jointly owning a pool could give everyone a lot of swimming for a relatively small cost. Again, consider the activities for which the pool will be used, where it could be placed, and how many people will use it. The same factors should be taken into consideration as previously mentioned. Figure out if a special cabana or dressing house with bathroom would be more suitable than using a home base. Will it also be more convenient to put in some kind of snack center?

This type of pool could present problems of neighborly cooperation. Multifamily pools work well only if you and your neighbors can come to an agreement on expenses and maintenance responsibilities. The best way to set up such a pool is through a corporation or homeowners' association. This legal entity can borrow money on its own for pool construction costs without the personal liability of individual members.

It is tougher to build a pool this way rather than a standard residential pool. There are a variety of health and building code legalities which must be dealt with. To arrange such a pool, contact a good lawyer. Some of the things you will want spelled out in writing are: How shall the pool be maintained? How will the costs be divided? What happens if someone doesn't pay? How should the property transfer be handled if one member moves and wants to give up his share?

Other Considerations For a family which plans much of its social life and entertainment around the swimming pool, one of the first questions to ask is: How much of the year can the pool be used? Enclosing or sheltering pools can often extend their use and may include the use of a pool heater. Privacy may be a key factor, and careful consideration should be given to ways and means of landscaping or fencing to give the necessary feeling of privacy.

The family that plans on a lot of poolside entertaining should take into account that it may need a larger than usual amount of terrace or deck space, underwater pool lights, gas lamps, external lighting, and electrical outlets.

Special family needs may sometimes mean planning for a therapeutic pool or spa. These pools are relatively shallow with underwater steps or another kind of sitting arrangement. They can be built separately from the main pool or as part of it, with a small dam separat-

A very limited area requires careful pool and landscape planning. This pool requires most of the available backyard space but is well situated to provide maximum out-door enjoyment. Fencing and trees provide privacy. Photo courtesy of National Swimming Pool Institute

Some pool owners prefer the pool to be near the house. With small children in the home this can be an extra precaution; and a well-done pool makes one of the most beautiful "living pictures" a home can have. Photo courtesy of Robert Crozier & Associates

Therapeutic pools or hot tubs can be beneficial and may be constructed separately from the pool, as above, or with a small dam separating the two units. Photo courtesy of Renaissance, Pompano Beach, Florida

Be careful when planning shallow swimming for children. Although a shallow end is needed, children outgrow it quickly. The shallow section at right works as an entrance into the water. Photo courtesy of National Swimming Pool Institute

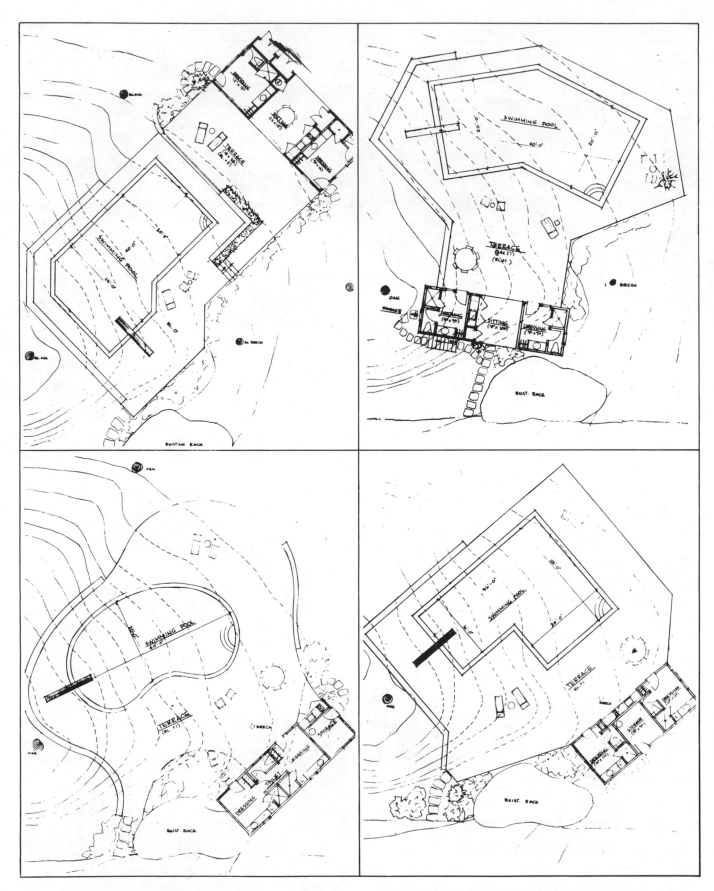

When planning your outdoor living room, alternatives abound. In presenting preliminary plans to a client, the architect will often do a series of sketches indicating differing pool placements, shapes, and arrangements. Drawings courtesy of Robert Crozier & Associates

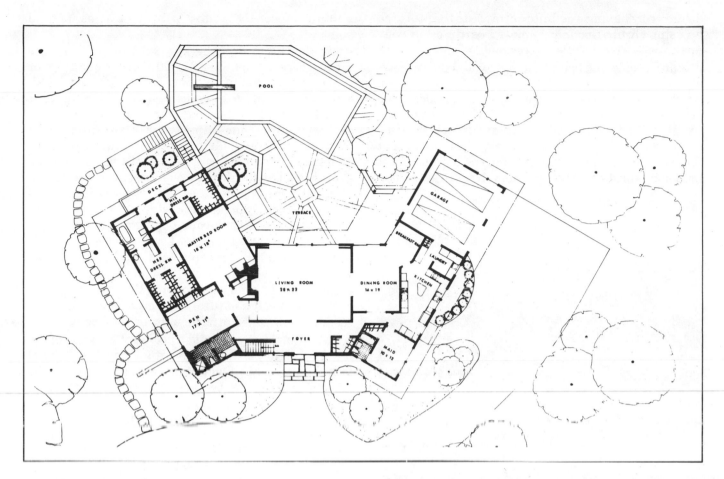

ing the two units. In the typical therapeutic pool, hydro-air jets below the surface of the water cause the water to move around the pool at a relatively high velocity and massage individuals seated in the pool. A temperature control, either tied in with the main pool or controlled separately, allows you to heat the water to a desired temperature.

Carefully consider how much time you and your family are willing to give to maintaining the pool properly. Unfortunately, a pool does not maintain itself. How much time will be given before the effort becomes such a chore that the pool falls into disuse?

You can work around your pool vacuuming, hand skimming, and water purifying for an hour each day, saving money on equipment; or you can, by purchasing automatic equipment, reduce the time to one hour a week. An above-ground swimming pool requires about 15 minutes work per day, or you can do nothing, hiring instead a pool service which does the complete job for you.

Your Home and Surroundings

As you determine your family life-style needs, you should remember that the pool and its facilities should look like an outdoor room and be treated as one. This requires a three-dimensional effect, which can be

Although farther from the home, these pool designs still use the pool as a landscape focal point for inside viewers.

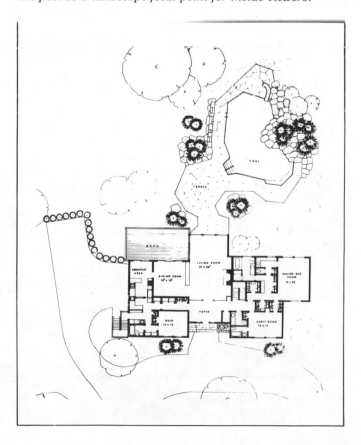

achieved by having a definite entrance to the pool area by using shrubs, mounds of moved earth (excavation dirt), rocks, trees, walls, fences, and so on.

Many people like to have their pool and the immediate surroundings directly outside their living room window as a three-dimensional living picture. This affords them the visual benefit of the pool and the feeling of being near water even at times of the year when swimming may be impossible. Others find that the pool suits them best away from the house, almost hidden by shrubs or other greenery. Nevertheless, it is

Backdrops of cities, mountains, or a golf course can help frame your pool and greatly enhance impact. Photo courtesy of National Swimming Pool Institute

still an outdoor living area with the pool as its focal point.

Looking natural is the key word in your outdoor room, whether you have a $2,000 above-ground pool or a $20,000 in-ground masterpiece. Landscape architects suggest landscaping the pool to achieve the most natural effect. If you are lucky enough to have a natural backdrop for your swimming pool, you can use it to frame the pool area. Mountains, golf courses, valleys, and even cityscapes increase a pool's visual impact. Pool placement should not look forced in an area where it might jar someone to see it. Its size, shape, and elevation should blend naturally with the surrounding area. A rule of thumb for judging proper location is to imagine where a natural body of water would be located. This often means placing the pool in a low area where water would collect. If an elevated position is preferred or demanded by the site, there are a number of ways to give it a natural look rather than making it seem like an added afterthought to your home.

For example, if you build a pool in the middle of the lawn, it might be hard to give it a three-dimensional look, but it can be done. When you excavate for the pool, take the dirt and create mounds around the pool. These will become grassy slopes. They should slope toward the pool. If rocks are dug up, they can be used to hold the slope and also give the pool area even more visual interest. If the slope is done properly, you can hide the filter equipment behind it.

Shrubs, terraces, decks, and fences can help to achieve that three-dimensional effect for your outdoor living room. Often brick or natural-looking modular materials are more effective than concrete around the pool area. If you use black slate, tile, bricks, stones, or patio blocks, you can plant low shrubs or grass between them for a pleasing effect.

Disinfectants in the water such as chlorine, iodine, or bromine can damage plant life. Where a lot of splash-out takes place, it might be best to widen decks and use potted plants and shrubs. Another idea is to

Formal landscaping with higher growth away from pool helps to frame an outdoor room. Photo courtesy of National Swimming Pool Institute

raise the planting area a foot or two above the pool level.

An above-ground pool can present a landscape problem; it is an unnatural body of water. When building this type of pool, try to locate it so that it is on the side of a hill. This allows one side of the pool to be close to the ground. Plantings and decks around above-ground pools can aid in giving a natural, three-dimensional look.

To blend the pool into its surroundings, there is no reason why the shape of the pool must be rectangular. If a free-form, circular, kidney, teardrop, or L-shaped pool would seem more suitable to the landscape, they are all available today. Historically, pools were rectangular because they were all constructed of poured concrete. The bottom slab was poured and then the sidewalls were poured. But with today's technology you need not limit yourself to a rectangular pool.

Although many people think a rectangular pool is best for exercise, this is not the case. You don't need a rectangular pool for swimming laps as long as you have two contiguous walls. What you then have is a rectangle inside a free-form pool. Also, if a free-form pool is to be used, the terrace, deck, or flat area around it does not have to follow the exact lines of the pool. In fact, the area might look better and more natural if it

Pools can be practically any shape. Photo courtesy of National Swimming Pool Institute

doesn't. At the shallow end of the pool the terrace may be larger, because people tend to congregate there as they come out. At the deep end, the terrace need only be 2 feet wide, since this may be for access only.

There is nothing more natural than a tree near water, as long as it does not interfere with the diving, sun, or upkeep of the pool. This may sound like a tall

Various structures enclosing a pool can help expand its use from two months more a year to all-year-round. Photo courtesy of National Swimming Pool Institute

The rectangle is a basic and generally inexpensive pool shape. Photo courtesy of National Swimming Pool Institute

order for a tree, but white birches and similar trees work exceptionally well around pools and give a dramatic effect. If you are really interested in placing trees near the pool, it is best to consult a landscaper or a person who works in a tree nursery. You must be sure the trees' spread and root systems will not interfere with the piping system.

Some pool owners prefer deciduous trees because they have only one big leaf fall, and then it is over. A pool cover can be used at this time of year to prevent leaves from fouling the pool. The small continuous leaf drop of evergreens and conifers can create maintenance problems. Fruiting shrubs, obviously, should be kept well away from the pool area. The falling fruit can stain decking and attract bees or other stinging insects.

Striving for the natural effect, many landscape architects claim that the most natural water tone can be achieved by painting the inside of the pool black. This gives water a green tint and reflects objects near the pool. In a black pool, light is reflected off the water's surface rather than absorbed.

If you wish a more blue than green look to the water, paint the pool white. This gives it more of a blue tone than does blue paint. Gray paint creates a green tint, while the most popular color, blue, actually gives the least natural tone to the water.

Decking need not extend completely around the pool to be effective, but it must be well planned. Photo courtesy of National Swimming Pool Institute

Larger trees and fencing set this pool off but do not keep the sunlight out. Photo courtesy of California Redwood Association.

Practical Ideas

Before you start dreaming yourself into some pretty deep water where swimming pools are concerned, consult the experts. You and your family may understand your needs and be able to speak intelligently with the professionals, but you'd be more than wise to get their advice on how to balance your dreams with your pocketbook and your property limitations.

The Experts

There are a number of ways to get in touch with reliable swimming pool professionals in your area.

You can find a regional chapter of the National Spa and Pool Institute (NSPI) by contacting the main office at 200 K Street N.W., Washington, D.C. 20006. As a nonprofit trade association for the swimming pool industry, your best interests will be served by this group. The members seek to maintain high standards, so that poor equipment or shady deals won't be sold to an uninformed pool-buying public. The NSPI can recommend reputable builders, dealers, and designers in your area. The organization also gives minimum standard requirements for residential pools, and if your pool is built according to its standards, you can register your pool with NSPI. The regional office may even offer advice about financing.

To find reputable pool builders and dealers, consult satisfied pool-owning friends who have dealt with local pool contractors. To get in touch with landscape architects or residential architects, ask for recommendations from the NSPI or satisfied pool owners. You should be aware that not every professional architect designs swimming pools.

A landscape architect wears only one hat—planning and design. If you choose to use one, he or she will plan and design your pool to exact specifications. The architect can recommend several competent pool contractors or dealers in your area. Once you have selected your builder, the landscape architect will visit your pool site regularly to make sure his plans and specifications are being followed. This guarantees a quality job.

Should you wish to become a owner-builder, the landscape architect will suggest good area subcontractors for electrical, plumbing, and excavation work. Regardless of where you get your leads, it is your responsibility to check out the company or companies yourself. Your money is being spent, and it is up to you to protect it and get the best buy for your dollar.

Once you have chosen the people with whom you will work, call the Better Business Bureau in your community. This organization cannot tell you if the company is good, bad, or indifferent; but it will inform you of the number of complaints against it. Above all, ask for references. In the case of a landscape architect, for instance, references are his or her lifeblood. The same goes for the reputable pool builders and dealers. Obviously, these professionals cannot give you a list of every person for whom they have done work, but they can furnish you with a cross section of customers. Those that hesitate or refuse to give you references should be dropped immediately.

What to Avoid

A lucrative and growing field such as the pool business attracts unscrupulous dealers and builders, but these people can be identified. According to the NSPI you should watch out for:

- unauthorized free-lance salespersons who want you to sign contracts and then peddle them to the lowest bidding contractor;
- bargain prices and salespersons who say you will get a special price because your pool is to be a model used for advertising purposes;
- salespersons who ask for a check made out to them or for cash rather than a check made out to the company, or ask for full payment in advance;
- salespersons who ask you to sign a contract in blank or a contract that does not cover all representations he has made orally;
- salespersons who offer to save you money by helping you build your pool (they may be taking under-the-counter rebates from the materials supplier).

If you come across any of the above-mentioned people, you should report them immediately to both the Better Business Bureau and the NSPI in Washington.

Site Location

There are general rules which may help you and the builder or landscape architect choose the location of the pool in relation to your house and property lines. It must be stressed that many of these rules can and should be ignored if they do not apply to your project. This is where expert judgment is most important.

You should be sure to discuss the following items:

1. drainage around the pool;

2. excavation details;
3. amount of sunlight;
4. protection against wind;
5. trees and plantings;
6. poolside space.

This is an outstanding example of how a swimming pool can be combined with the site. The pool is away from the house, but because of lower elevation, it is still in view. Photo courtesy of National Swimming Pool Institute

Drainage Your pool site should have good surface and subsurface drainage away from the pool. Good surface drainage helps maintain a clean pool and prevents dirty water from washing back into the pool from the immediate surrounding area. It also keeps your decks from getting wet and slippery. In poor drainage areas, the coping or lip of your pool can be raised to keep water out.

Subsurface drainage is another problem entirely, and you should be continuously aware of it. The big problem is that subsurface water exerts hydrostatic pressure against your pool walls. Should enough pressure be exerted against smooth concrete walls, it can cause them to crack, split, or "float" (rise out of the ground) when the pool is empty. Once the pool is in place, the problem of hydrostatic pressure can be overcome by keeping the pool filled all year around. The immediate weight of the water counterbalances the ground water pressure.

Site planners frequently try to avoid low-lying areas. If you are new in your neighborhood, you might inquire what the biggest rainstorms did over the last 10 to 20 years. Your pool site might very well be situated where 5 feet of water collects during storms. Obviously, you should avoid that site.

Drainage can sometimes be a problem, particularly when the pool is located near a larger body of water. Always seek professional advice in situations like this before committing yourself to any particular type of pool. Photo courtesy of Rule Aquatech Pool Company

Coping is raised slightly above deck area and a block is placed around it to allow for easy drainage and to prevent water from flowing back into pool. Photo courtesy of National Swimming Pool Institute

Sometimes situating your pool on a site which has poor subsurface drainage cannot be avoided. This is especially true of swimming pools built near oceans or lakes. If possible, a good pool contractor can direct all or most of the water away from the immediate pool area by using underground drainage pipes (much like a leeching field), dry wells, or simply by grading the land.

Excavation Details Not even the most expert landscape architect or pool builder will always be able to tell whether or not you will have site problems. Potential problems must be investigated and then evaluated in great detail. For instance, you might set aside $300 or $500 for your swimming pool excavation (first, find out if you are being charged by the day or for the completed job). If you run into any one of a number of difficulties, excavation costs may increase substantially. Site excavation costs can increase because of major problems with water, rock, or sandy soil.

Water can present several problems. A contractor might specify that he will install pumps capable of removing 75 gallons a minute from the excavation; but if you have additional water flowing in, you will be charged for the extra machinery and labor required to keep the site dry while construction is underway. It is possible to keep almost any site dry, but it can be very expensive. One Connecticut pool contractor once kept Long Island Sound out of the excavation while a pool was being constructed. Obviously, these people must keep the pool full all year round to counteract the hydrostatic pressure.

Rock may be a big problem in your area. Anyone you

deal with should be willing to make a test boring of your site if rock formation is suspected. Often rock might be apparent a few feet underground. If it is detected in time, the pool can be constructed around it, and perhaps it can even be used to advantage, as part of the landscaping or one of the walls of the swimming pool. If rock cannot be avoided, blasting may be necessary. Unless you have a lot of money to spend, you should try to avoid bringing an explosives expert on the site. He may charge $50 per yard of rock removed. If this doesn't sound like much to you, there is also a minimum charge of $1,800 for coming on the site.

Sandy soil becomes a problem because the excavated pool walls may cave in after digging has progressed beyond a certain point. To prevent this, extra machinery and materials are often brought onto the site to shore up the walls; this will, of course, increase your excavation costs.

Another consideration is the actual excavated dirt. It will cost you money to have it removed. By planning what to do with it at the same time the pool and surrounding area is designed, you might be able to use the dirt to good advantage and save money.

Now is also the time to check out any underground utility lines which may be in your pool site. Find out how much you will be charged to reroute them if the need arises.

Amount of Sunlight To take advantage of as

much sunlight as you can during swimming hours, it is possible to determine a site location that will best suit this purpose. Find out the yearly sun cycle and then the daily path of the sun during that cycle on your pool site. Begin by standing in various spots on your pool site, look straight to the south, and raise your eyes slightly to the angle where the sun's noon position should be. (Note the sunrises, sunsets, and angles of noon positions during the yearly cycles.) If you encounter an open sky, you will have sun on the spot where you now stand. If there are any obstructions such as trees or your house, the area will be in shade.

Keep in mind that from December 21 to June 21 the sun sets farther north each day. From June 21 to December 21 it sets farther south each day. Knowing the sunrise, sunset, and noon position of the sun (it is always slightly to the south), you can approximate the amount of sunlight on your pool site.

Most experts advise placing the pool in the sun on the assumption that this offers maximum enjoyment and economy (because the sun heats the pool). This is not always true. Too much sun can be a problem in hot-weather climates, and the lack of privacy on a sunny site may override heating savings.

Protection Against Wind When choosing your

Although the pool is surrounded by large trees which add drama to the setting, it is well situated to gain a maximum amount of sun during the afternoon, the most popular swimming hours. Photo courtesy of American Plywood Assn.

site, seriously consider the wind. While it may not be bothersome during the summer months or in the middle of the day, as the days cool down during the spring and autumn, the wind could discourage any serious swimming. It also causes heat loss from the water, which makes your heater work harder and your utility bills go higher.

Strong winds can cause other problems. Carried on virtually every wind are dust and debris. In the air it may not make much of a difference, but in your pool it will cause more work and maintenance for you.

A site with a natural windbreak is probably the most economical protection against the wind. Placing the pool in a good position in relation to your house or a special land configuration may act as a natural wind barrier. A natural windbreak can also be created from the dirt excavated from the hole. Another way to deal with the problem at the planning stage is to consider thick, fast-growing plantings, fences, a canvas backdrop, or the like. Wind protection usually pays off in more ways than one.

There are three types of winds which may affect your pool site: prevailing winds, localized seasonal breezes, and high velocity winds. Prevailing winds, in most cases, will influence your pool site more than the others. Often, it is the wind-chill factor which will make you feel that it is 62 degrees Fahrenheit because of a 10 mph wind blowing directly on you when it may be 4 to 8 degrees warmer. Or under the same 10 mph

Where natural windbreaks are not available, various types of fencing can reduce wind problems while giving you a greater degree of privacy. Photo courtesy of the American Plywood Association

The wind can create chill and dust problems. This pool's owner has skirted the problem by using a natural windbreak of vegetation. Photo courtesy of National Swimming Pool Institute

wind, sunny placement and pool shelters can make you feel 8 to 10 degrees warmer than the original 68 degrees Fahrenheit.

Local weather information on the direction of winds at your pool site can often be found in U.S. Weather Bureau offices, National Park Service and ranger stations, U.S. Coast Guard stations and district offices, public power and utility companies and water districts, city or county or state road and highway maintenance departments, and Federal Aviation Administration branches and local airports.

Trees and Plantings As discussed earlier, it is not usually advisable to plan your pool near large trees. Cleaning problems arise due to falling leaves and seeds, and the trees may shade the pool too much for maximum use. The site planner can advise you if trees or other plantings offer a drawback to a site.

Poolside Viewing Look at your pool site carefully with the expert and figure out what your pool will look like, if visible, from your house. Will the glare from the rising or setting sun on the pool blind your family when you all sit down to breakfast or supper? One thing you might do is to roughly mark out the area where your pool will be and live with it for a while. In this way you can also find out if access to the pool is awkward. If your original site choice proves inconve-

nient, mark out other areas until you are satisfied.

Privacy and space around the pool are two key factors to your long-term satisfaction with it. If the pool is not naturally secluded, find out ways you can make it so and how much it would cost. It may mean a good fence, or it may mean moving the pool to another spot.

Space Needs   What you plan to do around the pool determines the amount of space you need. If the pool is only for an occasional swim or for one or two people, a small amount of space will probably be adequate. If you intend to entertain at poolside, you'd better plan enough terrace or decking at the outset.

Limited space, not only for the pool itself but for the surrounding area activities, often seems an unavoidable problem, but you may not see all the location possibilities on your property the way an expert would. There are many fine examples of unusual usage such as locating a pool immediately adjacent to the house, or tucking it around a corner or into an unused, awkward piece of land. Keep an open mind to all suggestions, and you may be surprised at the results.

This is also the time to discuss any structures that you might want to incorporate now or in the future. If you want a cabana or change-room installed two years from now, make sure you have enough space now. Also, carefully consider placing your pool equipment where it does not interfere with your activities.

Hillside Pools   Not every site can be adapted for swimming pools. On the other hand, a piece of ground may look too rough or steep yet it can be suitable for a pool. This is the case with many hillside locations. To many designers and engineers, the hillside is often the best spot. It usually offers a more visually interesting and natural site and frequently has good subsurface drainage.

If you live on a hillside and would like a swimming pool built there, a number of possibilities are viable. You can cut a shelf in the hill and safely place an above-ground pool on it. Similarly, a cut-and-fill operation can make the downside slope strong enough to support a variety of in-ground pools. Another alternative is to use shoring or a retaining wall. If the soil of your hillside tends to be loose, you could install an in-ground steel pool which has self-supporting walls.

Expert Advice on Size and Shape

The size and shape of your pool may very well be influenced by your site plan. Keep in mind that anywhere from a 15 by 30-foot pool to a 20 by 40-foot pool is the average. This refers to a rectangular shape. If you plan a kidney shape, a 20 by 40-foot pool will be 20 feet at the widest point and a few feet smaller at the neck. Check into pool shape variations and make sure you have enough swimming space as well as land space. At the same time find out if a pool in an unusual shape

When planning diving facilities, plan adequate space around the board. Also situate the board so that reflection from the water does not blind the diver during the afternoon. Photo courtesy of National Swimming Pool Institute

will cost more. If it lessens excavation problems, it may save money.

For pools with diving facilities, you should be aware that 8 to 10 feet of extra decking is needed on the diving end. You may also wish to discuss placing the diving board or deep end at the point farthest from the house for safety purposes. You do not want divers to be blinded by facing into the sun as they dive.

Planning for Extras

Certain extras for your pool should be planned for now, even if you actually purchase the items later. Other extras can never be added once your pool is completed.

You may not be able to add on a diving board if the pool's depth is too shallow. A ladder, set in the deck with anchors, must be planned before the pool is constructed. The same applies, obviously, to recessed pool steps.

It is much more expensive to add on such things as underwater lights or a pool heater once the pool is finished. Find out from your pool designer or builder for which extras it is worthwhile to plan. Can a cabana wait as long as the land is always there for you to use? Should you landscape immediately? What about extra electrical wiring or an outside gas light?

Sit down and ask the expert about every single item your family feels it needs and can afford for its dream pool. You and the professional can figure out if it pays to wait or to delete it completely from your plans.

Materials Used in Pools Your in-ground pool, if it is 20 by 40 feet, will hold 30,000 gallons of water, weighing over 124 tons! That's a heavy problem to contend with if the pool has not been planned right.

Reliable expert advice on the best type of pool material for construction of your pool is invaluable. With the variety of choices now on the market, you would be in over your head if you tried to make a decision based on your knowledge, your neighbor's knowledge, or on cost alone.

There are five basic types of materials that can form the foundation or shell for your pool. The experts can guide you on which is best suited for your climate, most available in your area, and best for your site. These basic materials are concrete, fiberglass, steel, aluminum, and wood. Concrete in pool construction comes in various forms and construction systems. There is gunite (sprayed), block, hand-applied, and poured. The interiors of concrete pools are usually plastered or painted, or both. Steel, fiberglass, aluminum, and wood act as sidewalls and support a vinyl liner inside the pool which actually holds the water. Today there are fiberglass pools on the market that are delivered and installed as a single unit.

Here are a few general guidelines to follow when discussing materials with your pool contractor or dealer.

Poured concrete pools with plaster or paint interiors may be more expensive due to some hand labor in setting the forms and the time involved in waiting for the concrete to set. You may be able to achieve almost any shape you want, but it might run into added expense. These pools generally come in limited shapes such as teardrop, rectangular, or kidney. Poured concrete pools are often best for extreme cold-weather freezing problems or poor subsurface drainage. The interior of the pool must be plastered or painted (in almost any color) before use and should be repainted or resurfaced every few years. Maintenance is high due to algae, which tends to cling on textured walls.

Gunite (sprayed concrete) with plaster or paint interiors is usually built more easily and more quickly than poured concrete. This, of course, lowers the cost. But not always. Expenses may be higher in areas where pool building is not done on any large scale because special equipment is needed for the sprayed concrete process. Because gunite is shot from a hose, it follows any shape you wish to excavate, and does so without any seams. The shapes of gunite pools are limitless and have actually been formed in the shape of mushrooms, guitars, or stars. Gunite, however, may not hold up well in very cold climates. It has a rough texture which must be hand-trimmed before painting or plastering. The interior should be repainted or resurfaced every few years. The same maintenance vigilance must be applied as for poured concrete, since algae clings to the walls.

Masonry blocks may require the manual labor of stacking blocks and then pouring of the concrete floor base. It may, however, be one of the cheapest methods in an area where few pools are built. Very little special machinery or equipment is necessary, and stacking the blocks is relatively easy. Masonry blocks function well in almost any climate. The shape of the pool, however, is severely limited to rectangles, L-shapes, or any other shape involving straight lines. To curve the pool requires at least a 10-foot radius. Masonry blocks require an interior waterproof finish before plaster or paint can be applied. Once the interior is prepared, it can be plastered or painted and should be kept up every few years. Maintenance on walls for algae, again, is time-consuming.

Vinyl liners can be used as a substitute if you choose not to waterproof the blocks. The vinyl liner is itself a waterproof skin fitted to pool size and supported by the pool's wall and base. The surface of masonry block must still be prepared. All rough spots which may cause wear and tear on the liner must be smoothed out. The liners require no paint or plaster finish, and no repainting. If they tear, they can be patched up economically.

Vinyl liners are most often used with aluminum, steel, or wood foundations. The liner is becoming more and more popular. About half the swimming pools now installed have vinyl liners. The price is usually less than the concrete-based pools due to easy and fast installation. Although you may not have the complete freedom of choice of shapes as in gunite pools, there is a tremendous variety now on the market and more seem to be available each year. These liners also come in a variety of colors.

Properly winterized, these pools can withstand temperatures down to 40 degrees below zero. Maintenance is kept to an absolute minimum. The smooth surface never needs resurfacing or painting, will not crack or chip, and is not affected or discolored by chemicals (unless they are misused and placed directly on the liner), and algae will not readily cling to the walls. The vinyl-lined pool also does not require draining. Today a good liner carries a ten-to-fifteen-year guarantee. The liner can be torn, so make sure that seams are perfectly bonded. If the liner does tear, it can be mended with a patch kit.

Steel frames for vinyl liners offer tremendous strength for problem areas such as hillsides or climates with heavy freezing. The cost is higher than a poured concrete pool, even though the installation time is much shorter. The shape is limited because panels, either curved or straight, are available in standard sizes and sections.

Aluminum frames for vinyl liners cost less than steel. Their strength below ground is excellent. They

Swimming pools constructed of concrete are the most durable. Depending on the concrete system used, the pool can be formed in a variety of shapes. Photo courtesy of National Swimming Pool Institute

do well in most climates, and you can get prefab panels or shells in a number of shapes.

Wood frames for vinyl liners must be specially treated but never creosoted because it will destroy the vinyl. The cost is less than aluminum with the same amount of shapes available.

Fiberglass one-piece shells are not nearly as expensive as steel frames with vinyl liners but are excellent in climates with severe winters. Shapes are somewhat limited. Shells are available in most parts of the country and delivered by trailer truck (subject to state and local highway restrictions) to the site after excavation. Maintenance is low because algae will cling to the smooth surface, with no painting or resurfacing necessary. Color is built into the material.

Fiberglass wall panels over a concrete floor is a combination with both advantages and disadvantages. The cost is about equal to a gunite pool; it is good in most weather conditions; the panels are flexible so the pool can be made into almost any shape. But the "easy maintenance" applies only to walls. The floor is finished with a masonry-type waterproof coating or is painted, which means resurfacing or repainting, plus a possible algae problem.

There are a number of materials used when finishing off your pool with coping and trim. Trim (usually tile or other easily cleaned material placed at the waterline where scum forms) and coping (the lip around the edge of the pool) are used mainly with concrete pools. Vinyl-lined pools and fiberglass pools

come with prefinished interiors with coping as part of the structure.

Tile for trim can be purchased in various sizes, shapes, and colors. Coping can be anything from precast concrete paving stones or brick to flagstones or other nonskid materials. You may eliminate coping if you want to extend your paving over the lip in order to blend the pool with your land configuration rather than having the pool well defined.

Quality Work at the Right Price

You should now have a good idea of the location, size, and building material for your swimming pool. The cost may vary according to the builder, market competition, the season, or the type of plan you desire. If you wish to use a landscape architect, your cost may be increased but your protection and design originality increase also. If you hire a contractor or builder to do the complete job, it may cost less, but you will probably devote more of your own time to the project.

You may also wish to work with the builder yourself on an owner-builder plan, thereby decreasing the cost further. You had better be sure that you can accomplish the jobs in a professional manner. Be very careful. Banks are often hesitant to give improvement loans on owner-builder pools because they feel the quality of the work may not be adequate.

Even with proper materials, you may never be able

to rectify a poor construction job without exorbitant rebuilding costs. Shop around for qualified and reliable experts. Look for people who will stand firmly behind their work.

Assuming that you have been discussing your pool with qualified people, ask them to submit bids making sure they are giving you equivalent materials in each case. One builder may offer a completed pool with all the trimming, but any variation from that particular pool will cost a great deal. Another builder may not have a "package" for you, and although the initial price is higher, after pricing the variations from the package you may find the package deal is not to your advantage. Again, an owner-builder plan may not be cheaper if you must arrange for the materials, labor, and equipment yourself. A contractor with sizeable volume may be able to do the complete job for you for less because of the lowered cost to him on materials, labor, and equipment.

A few ways to ensure that the builder of your choice will install a quality pool is to see if he has a licensed electrician on his staff or will hire one. If you desire landscaping, make sure the landscaper knows where the pipes and pool lines are located before he digs.

Each pool requires engineering structural drawings for its own site plan. Make sure you have them. It might pay to visit a structural engineer to check the soundness of your pool's structure. It will take less than an hour and cost about $75 to $100.

You also may wish to consult the NSPI and have the builder register the pool with them. Any NSPI builder can participate in the Pool Registry Program. This ensures that your pool conforms to the NSPI's suggested minimum standards for residential pools. These standards include classification of residential pools into several types, determined primarily by the safety ratio of pool depth, width, length, and diving hopper configuration. It also ensures that your pool is designed and constructed according to NSPI standards. When completed, your pool is registered with an agent of the NSPI in Washington, D.C., according to type and number.

The Contract

Once you have chosen a builder to install your pool, and both of you agree on all the points mentioned, you are ready to go to contract. Never sign any contract under pressure, and be sure all issues are firmly decided in writing before you sign. Builder members of the NSPI use a uniform contract which is adjusted to your state and local requirements. It should provide maximum protection for the customer. Have your lawyer check the contract before you sign. Under any circumstances, all contracts should cover the following in detail:

1. Expenses for materials and labor should be itemized, including optional equipment and accessories, and who pays for each.
2. Brand names of equipment such as filters, plumbing, and heating, and exact grades, weights, styles, and colors of all materials used.
3. Exact specifications of your pool size, shape, and depth, along with a complete detailed description of the pool structure, dimensions, and location on your lot (this should include piping lengths and square footage of patios and paths).
4. When the work will be started and when it will be completed.
5. An agreement concerning the procedures and charges for plan modifications by the owner during construction.
6. Unusual or extra costs and who pays for them, such as moving electrical, water, or gas lines, rock blasting, and utility hookups.
7. Full cost of the pool, if financed.
8. Very clear cancellation provisions.
9. Fully outlined warranty and guarantee of pool structure (including vinyl liner), equipment (pump and filter), accessories—what the warranty and guarantees cover, for how long, and under what conditions—who is responsible for servicing and repairing, and how it is to be done.
10. Clearly defined schedule of payments to builder, the final one to be made after the pool has been completed and is in proper operating order, with agreement on who fills the pool and starts up the equipment.

Once construction starts, you may want to check the accuracy of the work. After working hours or on weekends, you can measure the dimensions of the excavation pool site and see if they tally with the plan figures. You can also check the materials without interrupting the work.

To be sure that you are meeting payments for work actually being performed and for materials and equipment and accessories actually purchased according to the specifications and the contract, speak with the builder or landscape architect. By maintaining a good working relationship you will earn the respect of the professionals and avoid the less than desirable results that can occur if they think the owner is unconcerned.

Using Solar Energy to Heat Your Pool

The use of solar energy for heating homes, domestic hot water supplies, and swimming pools has gained new respect and popularity in recent years. Even as this new technology becomes more commonplace, the fact is there is really nothing new or revolutionary about these systems. Most of what is in use today is a take-off on technology which has been around for decades or even longer. It merely took escalating fuel prices to make these systems more attractive and economically feasible.

A solar heating system for your pool may or may not fill your needs. If your main intent is to save money on energy, you might consider putting a clear plastic cover over your pool anytime it is not in use. When the pool has a clear cover and is exposed to the full sun, it is in itself a solar heating system which can easily bring water temperature about 10 degrees above air temperature. If you add windbreaks around your pool to discourage heat loss, the pool water may reach a slightly higher temperature.

On the other hand, if you enjoy water temperatures which are 20 to 30 degrees warmer than air, (and can afford the expense), you might do well to go with a conventional fossil fuel or electric pool heater. You should still incorporate a pool cover to help modify your costs somewhat.

If you fall somewhere in the middle and would enjoy warmer water, which is perhaps 15 degrees warmer than the air temperature, you can achieve this with a solar heating system and a good cover over the pool.

A conventional heater will heat your pool to the desired temperature in several days. A solar heating system will heat your pool in seven to ten days, so long as you have a string of clear, sunny days. A conventional heater is priced from $600 to over $1,000 and could cost anywhere up to several hundred dollars a month in fuel bills, depending on the size of your pool and how much you run the heating system.

A solar heating system, on the other hand, can cost as little as a few hundred dollars up to $10,000, depending on the size and complexity of the system. Generally speaking, however, a solar heating system for an average-size swimming pool will cost from $2,500 to $4,000 for a contractor-installed and guaranteed system.

A conventional heating system never pays for itself. A solar heating system will pay for itself in saved fuel bills in a few years.

A solar heating system is a good substitute, but it is not exactly a replacement. A properly sized system will give you warm water, depending on weather conditions, but it can't give you really warm water the way a conventional system can unless the solar heating system is very extensive.

If you don't mind spending the money, a conventional heating system can extend your swimming season from very early spring to very late autumn. If you don't mind wasting energy and a lot of money, you could probably keep the pool heated all winter. A solar system will extend the season in the spring by about 25 percent, and by about 15 to 20 percent in autumn.

Solar Heating Systems

Solar heating systems, even the most complex for space heating, are still simple devices. There is a collector to capture the sun's rays, a system for transporting that heat, and a storage area for holding that heat until it is used. Solar heating systems for swimming pools are even simpler than the devices used for heating a house or the domestic hot water within that house. That's because there is a collection system and a transport system, but no storage medium—the pool serves that function. Another reason a solar heating system for a pool is relatively simple is because it does not have to make water hot; it merely has to raise the temperature of water a few degrees. In fact, heat requirements for a swimming pool fall into the lowest temperature stratum of any system.

The greatest benefit of a solar heating system is that once the system is installed and functioning properly, all the heat for your pool is free. Further, the greatest amount of solar energy for heating the pool will be available just when you want to do your swimming the most—on hot, bright, sunny days.

Deciding on a System Before you commit yourself to a solar heating system, there are a number of things to consider: Do you mind waiting a week for the pool to warm up? Can you swim in slightly warmer water or do you need the higher temperatures obtainable with a conventional system? Should you do it yourself or have a contractor do it? Unless you are experienced with plumbing and pipe fitting and can calculate heat gain and loss, you should allow someone else to do it. Ultimately, if you get a fair price from a reasonable contractor, that job will wind up costing you a lot less than if you try to do it yourself and encounter problems. If you do have the necessary skills, you can save money by designing and constructing your own solar heating system. Parts are available at your local home center or hardware store.

A simple system which you could build yourself, for example, would be to fasten lengths of black plastic hose to your roof or another area which has good southern exposure. Then, with the use of a small pump, you could pump cool water out of the pool into the hose where it would be heated on sunny days and then pump it back into the pool. The principle here is the same as a garden hose left in the sun. If you turn on that hose for watering, you will notice the first water out of the hose is really hot and then cools off as the tap water flows through. The catch is that just a little water will not adequately raise the temperature of your pool water. In fact, for an average-size pool, you would want to pump the entire volume of water through that hose in 12 hours. That means you would have to size a system properly in order to get a flow rate of about 30 gallons per minute. This type of system should be designed and constructed by a knowledgeable person. It's not a job for an amateur.

There are other things to consider as well before you commit to solar. What type of system is most efficient and least expensive for your exact location? Do you need to pay for a special structure on which to mount your collectors, or will your house roof or garage roof be adequate?

Can you obtain insurance on such a system? An insurance company with no experience in this area might refuse to insure it. If you install such a system without bothering to tell them, they might not cover it, should it be damaged. You also should consult with your building inspector in case there are any special code requirements.

While you can probably answer many of these questions yourself, you should consult with an architect with experience in this area or with a reliable contractor who installs these systems. Many swimming pool contractors now install these systems routinely. If they do not, they generally have a subcontractor with which they work.

Before deciding to go with a particular contractor, get the names of customers in your immediate area where the contractor has installed such a system. You not only need to take the usual precautions on hiring a competent workman, but you also should find out if a solar system is satisfactory in your area. The amount of sunshine varies greatly from area to area.

There is another alternative which you might like to consider. You can use a solar system and a conventional fossil fuel system. The fossil fuel system will raise the temperature rather quickly, and the solar system, with a clear cover, will help maintain that temperature.

Other alternatives might fit in well with your individual situation. In recent years, according to the how-to magazines on the newsstand, homeowners have been successfully heating their pools by cooling the air conditioning or heat pump coils in the pool. That is, on a hot summer day, all the heat that is being removed from your house by the air conditioner goes into heating your pool, rather than being lost in the air.

A rather sophisticated solution to cooling your house and heating your pool could be achieved with the inclusion of a heat pump. A heat pump works like an air conditioner in the summer, but in the winter, that same heat pump will draw heat out of chilly air and bring it into the house. If a heat pump is used with a swimming pool, the hot air in the summer is drawn out of your house and put into your pool. In the winter, that chilly water in the swimming pool still contains a tremendous amount of heat, and the heat pump could use that to heat your house. If such a system is not totally adequate in itself, a solar heat system could be used as a supplemental source.

How a Solar System Works

The solar heating system for a pool is quite simple. Water is pumped out of the pool and into the collectors of the system. The sun's rays are absorbed by that collector and heat the fluid within the unit. That fluid then moves out of the collector and back into the pool. Cooler pool water is continually pumped through the system to be heated.

The most common type of collector is the flatplate collector generally placed on the roof of the house or in the yard. The components of this type of collector include a transparent cover, a collector plate, (also called an absorber plate), and channels or piping.

The transparent cover is clear plastic or glass which allows the sun's rays into the unit, but inhibits their escape. If a cover were not included as part of the collector, a substantial amount of solar energy would be immediately lost, particularly on a windy day. The overall efficiency of a collector unit is greatly enhanced with a cover.

Once the rays of the sun penetrate the cover, they strike the absorber plate. Some of the radiation is absorbed, and some is reflected back out of the unit. To make the unit as efficient as possible, the plate is generally painted a dark color.

Another element of a solar heating system is the storage medium. When a system is constructed to help heat the house or domestic hot water, a substantial storage system is needed. With a swimming pool, as previously mentioned, the pool itself is the storage medium, thus eliminating much of the cost of the system.

What to Look For When Buying a System

There are many systems available on the market today. Most companies in this business have specific packaged systems for heating domestic hot water or swimming pools. As previously mentioned, the transparent cover can be either glass or plastic. Glass holds up longer than plastic and remains transparent longer. Glass, however, can be broken by vandals or by small tree limbs which might hit the collector during a storm. Therefore, you might want to use a plastic cover. Try to secure test reports on the life cycle of the plastic cover from the supplier with whom you are dealing. The main points to consider are resistance to breakage and long-term transparency.

The best absorber plates are those which are coated rather than painted. Through a process termed selective surfaces, this coating has a much higher efficiency for absorbing the sun's rays.

Two ways you lose heat once it enters the cover is through convection and radiation. Loss of heat by convection is simply the transfer of heat through the air. Radiation, of course, is the reflection of the sun's rays back through the cover. To make collectors more efficient, many companies use double thickness covers of either glass or plastic. This system is more expensive, but it further reduces heat loss and increases the efficiency of the overall system.

Regardless of the exact type of collector you would purchase for use in heating your swimming pool, it must be well constructed to be efficient. Besides having elements to retain the sun's rays once inside the collector unit, the unit itself must be very weathertight. Part of a well-constructed solar collector is the addition of insulation on the back of the unit. Fiberglass insulation 3 to 4 inches thick is excellent for this purpose.

The more efficient your collection system, the more heat it will be able to absorb and use to heat your swimming pool. There always will be some heat loss, but the amount depends on how efficient and how well-constructed a system you buy.

The flatplate collector is the most common and most expensive system for heating a swimming pool. In your local market, however, you might find a number of other systems available. The key to selecting any system for a swimming pool is that you must be able to have a substantial supply of warm water rather than a small supply of hot water. A small quantity of water flowing into your pool at 120 degrees Fahrenheit will

Solar panels located on the roof of the nearby structure supply heat for the swimming pool. Photo courtesy of Burke Solar Heater

not do nearly as much good as a large quantity of water heated only four or five degrees.

One of the easiest and least expensive systems to install is the so-called trickle collector, which can be fabricated from locally available materials. The pool water is pumped to a perforated pipe located at the top of the heat collector. This water then trickles down over a black plastic or metal sheet where it is warmed. Often a cover is used over this device to prevent evaporation. Once the water is at the bottom of this heat collector, it is allowed to flow through a pipe or gutter and back into the pool. A number of companies manufacture this type of collector system for pools.

There also are plastic rigid sheet collectors. In this case, two pieces of plastic, generally 4 by 8 feet or 4 by 10 feet, are bonded together. In this type of collector, the water from the pool is pumped from the bottom to the top and absorbs the sun's heat from the plastic as it rises. Once at the top of the unit, the warmer water flows back into the pool.

Another relatively simple system uses black plastic pipe attached to the roof or another area exposed to the sun. Water is pumped through the system and heated, then returned to the pool. There are many commercial variations of this on the market. Sometimes the plastic pipe is covered with a clear plastic surface and attached at the back to insulation board.

Water Ways

Now that the basic pool has been planned and your site chosen, the finishing touches that make it a family recreation center still remain. Often, these finishing touches can become very expensive.

There are several ways to save some money on your swimming pool, but some aspects of the job, such as plumbing or electrical wiring, might be too risky to do on your own. You might jeopardize the large investment of your swimming pool unless you have had previous experience in these areas.

Most of the items mentioned in this chapter are for the pool proper, such as aquaslides or pool enclosures, and while some may be considered necessities, others are completely optional. By exercising careful judgment, you will be able to meet your budget. There are a few ways to save money. Time can save you money. If you purchase your pool in an off season (usually the winter months), the pool may cost less than at peak seasons of spring and summer. Again, if you're building a house, ask about installing a swimming pool at the same time. Much of the heavy equipment is already on the site along with the masons, electricians, and other laborers. You may want to get the basic work done on a patio or barbecue when the men are there installing your pool. Having jobs done simultaneously will save money.

If you wish to keep a tighter rein on your budget there are builders who offer plans for building the pool in the fall and finishing up the interior and filling the pool in the spring. With this plan, you pay two-thirds of the cost in the fall and the balance in the spring when the pool is completed.

Added Features

There is a range of prices for the following pool items; you can decide where and how you want to invest the majority of your funds according to your particular needs or desires.

Heater Heating equipment can be one of your most expensive features costing about 12 to 14 percent of the pool price. The styles (direct or indirect heater) will influence the price. Your equipment company or contractor can show you the various advantages of different models and recommend one able to suit your pool setup and size. Operating costs may run anywhere from $50 to more than $100 a month.

Heaters and heating systems vary greatly. The three basic heaters are gas (natural and propane), electric, and fuel oil.

A gas heater, either natural or propane, costs less to install than a fuel oil heater and is normally cheaper to run than an electric system. One problem that has developed with gas is that many states have now instituted partial or complete gas bans with regard to swimming pools. Even though there is at present a more than adequate supply of the fuel, states have passed laws forbidding utilities to make new hookups to either swimming pool heaters or to outdoor decorative gas lamps. Your contractor can tell you what is happening in your area.

An electric system is only practical from a cost standpoint if your house is already heated electrically or if your local gas utility has imposed a moratorium on new gas hookups. You must also be certain that your electric house service can adequately handle the additional load of your pool heater.

Heaters using fuel oil are the least expensive to operate although they cost more for initial installation. Most give off a little smoke and odor and are noisier than the other systems.

Even though there are a number of solar heaters on the market, initial installation costs are often prohibitive, running into thousands of dollars. Of course, the fuel then costs you absolutely nothing. Rapid advances

The total swimming pool effect comes as much from the finishing touches as from the money spent building it.

Underwater lighting in watertight sockets illuminates the surface of this handsome pool, creating a relaxing reflecting pool. Colored lights, such as blue or green, would intensify the beauty. Photo courtesy of General Electric Company

are being made in this area, and within a few years a solar heating system for your pool could very well be both reliable and competitively priced.

A heater is an expensive feature. If you have planned for installation of a heater and have not yet made the actual purchase, you may wish to wait and see how your family enjoys the water as it is. The pool may be very well protected from winds and already warmed by the sun, so that the addition of a heater would be an unnecessary expense. Of course a heater can add to yearly use of the pool in the cooler months or at earlier and later hours of the day.

Diving Board If you have planned the depth and extra decking so that a diving board can be installed, you can count on spending anywhere from $200 to more than $400 for one. Probably a board of 10, 12, or 14 feet would be most practical. The least expensive board, made from laminated wood, is wrapped in fiberglass-reinforced plastic. The next board on the price list is made of high tensile laminated fiberglass cloth with rigid wood stringers. Both are durable and

have a built-in finish. The most permanent board, requiring the least upkeep, is made of extruded aluminum. If you don't have space for a diving board but your pool is deep enough, there are specially made shorter jump boards available.

Grab Rails and Ladders If your pool doesn't come with recessed steps, you may have planned for a ladder. It is set in the deck with anchors during the construction. Of the two materials from which ladders and hand grabs are made, chrome-plated brass is attractive and easily polished, but stainless is more durable. Depending on the number of treads and your choice of metal, the cost will vary.

Grab rails (shaped like the top of a pool ladder) go with recessed steps and are made of aluminum, stainless steel, or chrome-plated brass. There is less erosion on the grab rails than on ladders because the former are not immersed in water.

Aquaslide Children usually have a marvelous time with them. It may not pay to invest a great deal in this kind of optional accessory since it is usually out-

Indoor pools can offer you the opportunity to swim all year. Structures to house these pools are very expensive and can range up to $60 per square foot or more. Photo courtesy of Robert Crozier & Associates

grown by its users. Many are made with fiberglass runways and aluminum frames.

Underwater Lights This is an option which must be planned before the construction of the pool. Lights may cost you anywhere from $150 to more than $300, but about half of all pool owners have them. They are attractive at night and have the added safety factor of outlining the pool. There are also pool ladders that have lights built in. The lights must conform to your building code, and the electrician doing the work on the pool can advise you about low-voltage systems or others which the National Electrical Code has specified for pools. Bugs can be attracted by these lights.

Water Games and Floats These options can, of course, be purchased at your leisure or at your family's request. Snorkels, fins, and masks make excellent gifts for children. Water polo sets are always popular. You can also make your own games, races, or special items.

Pool Markers These optional ropes for shallow or deep-end use are made of polyethylene or nylon which is not affected by water. Plastic floats are generally attached at 3 or 4 foot intervals. The rope is fixed to hooks anchored in the side of the pool.

Pool Covers These are used to keep out debris and cut down on algae, and they come in a variety of materials and colors. Aside from vinyl or rigid motor-driven units, you can also use an inexpensive black polyethylene sheet to float over the water and anchor it at the poolsides with boards or rocks. It may not last more than two seasons.

Indoor Pools and Pool Enclosures

Building an indoor pool can mean home swimming all year, while pool enclosures can extend your swimming season from two months to all year, depending on the climate. It affords comfortable night or rainy-day swimming but is also relatively expensive.

An indoor pool can be added to an existing part of your house or added on as a new room or wing. This is the most expensive type of pool.

A major drawback to indoor pools is the greenhouse effect which tends to make the room very humid and uncomfortable while creating mildew and other housekeeping difficulties. Proper ventilation must be planned. When these rooms are ventilated in the winter, moist hot air is pumped out and cold air vented in. Some ventilators have heat recovery units so that moist air is pumped out but the heat is redirected back. If the room has a lot of glass, summer heat buildup will be considerable and a shading mechanism must be added.

Pool enclosures are available in many styles and price ranges. These units are constructed of wood or aluminum frames fitted with panels of fiberglass, plastic, or glass similar to that used in a greenhouse. The enclosures come in standard widths from 22 feet to 46 or 50 feet, and lengths are increased in 8 to 10 foot units.

Options on pool enclosures can include a heater (some owners simply rely on the heat from the pool) or sidewall and end panels which can be removed in warm weather. Screens are available to keep insects out.

Less expensive units are available such as a bubble that fits over your pool. But there is little or no provision made for humidity control, and swimming in this atmosphere is usually uncomfortable.

Cutting Pool Energy Consumption

Swimming pool energy costs can be expensive during the heavy-use season. A few simple procedures can cut these costs 40 to 50 percent. Most owners keep their pool heaters set around 82 degrees Fahrenheit.

The American Red Cross, however, says that a more healthful water temperature is 78 degrees Fahrenheit. That cut can save you about 40 percent of the energy you use for heating.

Other ways to save heater energy are to avoid frequent adjusting of the thermostat and to turn off the heater pilot light if the pool will be out of use for a week or longer. If the swimming pool is only used on weekends, the heater should be turned down at least 10 degrees during the week. Try to use the heater only during the early and late months of the season, which naturally extends swimming time. Well-sheltered pools can help here. Pool covers as well as windbreaks greatly reduce energy loss due to water evaporation.

One of the cheapest and most worthwhile purchases you can make is a time clock which turns the heater and filter on and off at selected hours. This can save a considerable amount of energy. One of the best clocks turns the heater off before shutting off the filtration system to prevent heat accumulating in the mechanism.

The filtration system, in fact, is probably operated too much in most pools. Experts say that in the typical residential pool the filter is operated ten to twelve hours and often longer. But even in peak periods of use the filter usually can do the job in six or seven hours. At nonpeak times the filtration system can be operated for even shorter periods.

Regular maintenance and cleaning of pump and filter will allow them to work more efficiently and to consume less energy. Maintenance of a properly conditioned and chemically balanced pool with a pH between 7.2 and 7.6 will also reduce energy consumption. When filtration time is reduced, it is especially important to maintain an adequate chlorine residual to keep the water safe for swimming.

Operating hours of the pool's automatic cleaner can be reduced from six or more hours to three or four hours a day which cuts energy by as much as 50 percent. Should the reduced operating hours of either the filter or the automatic cleaner allow the water to become murky, increase cleaning time in ½-hour intervals until sufficient time is allowed for proper cleaning.

As for lighting, pool and patio lights are often used for aesthetic rather than safety reasons. Lights can usually be safely reduced or turned off when the pool is not in use.

In-Ground Pool Construction Systems and Finishing

While many above-ground pools are designed with the do-it-yourselfer in mind, most in-ground pools are not. If you feel you must build the pool yourself to conserve the cost, you are limited to an above-ground pool. Another drawback is that most lending institutions will not make loans for swimming pools when people do the work themselves. Bankers contend that it is difficult enough to find a good in-ground pool contractor today to ensure quality work for their loans. A do-it-yourself job is usually out of the question when financing is involved.

A major problem for the amateur who tries to build an in-ground pool is that unintentional defects which creep into the work can cause maintenance problems and even pool failure. A good contractor knows what he is doing and will guarantee his work for a reasonable amount of time, generally about five years.

If you want an in-ground pool and are looking for ways to save dollars at the same time, do not look for shortcuts or money-savers in the pool structure. A long-lasting shell is where you should invest your money.

Site Excavation

On all in-ground pools, the site must either be dug up or filled in. While most sites must be dug, there are some sites that can accommodate a pool by filling in at least one side.

The ideal site on which to build a pool is free of water and underground debris yet has firm, well-packed soil. Few sites are ideal. To find out what kind of ground you have, it is wise to have the site thoroughly investigated at the planning stage. The usual method is to test the soil by taking borings about every 5 feet. A log or picture can be created which tells you the changes in stratum, water table, percentage of rock core recovery, characteristics and formations of rock, and all the irregularities of the substrata. This testing can eliminate unpleasant surprises later. In swimming pool construction, a surprise while excavating often means more money.

In most areas of the United States, three types of major soil problems, as well as some minor ones, can arise. Major problems involve loose soil such as sand, rock formations, and high water tables.

Pool Types and Their Construction

There is no type of in-ground pool construction system which is best, but rather one that is right for you and your site. On the market today are pools constructed of concrete, fiberglass, and metal or wood with vinyl liners.

Any well-constructed in-ground pool will last indefinitely. The exact life of any particular pool has not been accurately determined. A concrete pool, under the same circumstances, will last longer than a vinyl-lined pool. But when the liner goes, you can replace it. The four types of concrete construction systems available are poured concrete, block, hand-packed, and gunite.

Poured Concrete The poured concrete pool is one where forms are erected and concrete poured between them. This system has declined in popularity in recent years. The labor involved in setting up and tearing down forms is too costly in areas where gunite is available. At one time the shape of poured concrete pools was limited to variations of a rectangle. Today, you can get a kidney or teardrop shape as well. There are still severe limitations to concrete compared with gunite.

A series of wall forms are built of wood into which steel reinforcing bars are placed as specified by the pool engineer or designer. A wooden box is placed within these forms where holes are required for surface skimmers and drains. Special couplings used for inlets or vacuum lines are often filled with grease to prevent the entry of concrete. Once forms and steel are firmly in place, the concrete is poured and the form removed when the concrete sets. Then the floor is poured monolithically. Most contractors use more cement buildup on the corners and then trowel it evenly into a curve. Once all the concrete has set, the pool is very carefully backfilled with the excavated dirt.

A do-it-yourselfer should not attempt a poured concrete pool unless he has had extensive experience. The technologies involved in concrete walls are not nearly as simple as pouring a walkway or patio slab.

Masonry Block Masonry block pools have more potential for the do-it-yourselfer than any other type of concrete pool system. Although most big pool contrac-

This pool is designed to be viewed from many areas of the home. A deck overlooks the pool as well.

A covered patio adds to the convenience of this small but elegant pool. Close proximity and the view through sliding glass doors brings the pool's beauty to the inside entertainment area. Photo courtesy of Hedrich-Blessing

This pool (upper right) is built near the house so children can be supervised. Photo courtesy of Hedrich-Blessing

This prototype house and kidney-shaped swimming pool (lower right) are heated by solar panels located on the roof. The unit is a striking example of how we may efficiently heat pools in the near future. The decking is bleached redwood. Photo courtesy of Copper Development Association

Various types of pool enclosures can extend the swimming season of your pool. In colder climates you can add up to two months; in warmer areas swimming is possible all year. Photo courtesy of Catalina Aquatech

Pools with steel walls and a vinyl liner offer incredible strength and beauty. This type of pool goes well in areas with loose dirt or on hillsides. Photo courtesy of Heldor Associates

To give the pool area an "outdoor room" atmosphere, use fences and trees as framing devices. Photo courtesy of National Swimming Pool Institute

In this enclosed pool, the outside is brought inside by plantings flanking the structure. The structure acts as a greenhouse. Photo courtesy of Dick Keiser

This pool has been integrated with the traffic pattern of the residents. The sliding glass door offers a varied and lovely view from the living room. Photo courtesy of Hedrich-Blessing

Pool construction systems have advanced to the point that today you can have a fresh water pool right on a larger body of salt or fresh water. Here a vinyl liner is used. Photo courtesy of Aquatech, Fort Lauderdale

The use of natural rock, vegetation, and shape give this pool (above left) an exciting appearance that can be viewed from the entertainment area of the home. Photo courtesy of Armstrong and Sharfman

Accessories, such as the ladder, slide, and diving board (above right) should be considered in the initial plan and design. Photo courtesy of Heldor Associates

Plywood walls and a vinyl liner offer an outstanding construction value (lower right). Photo courtesy of the American Plywood Association

Good design can turn a problem site into an advantage. This pool features multilevel redwood decking. The photo above shows the pool-level deck at the deep end. The photo at right shows a casual outdoor dining area below pool level. Natural vegetation enhances this design. Photo courtesy of Armstrong and Sharfman

From a fully equipped eating area to lush vegetation, tile and geometric shapes give this pool its dramatic yet comfortable look. Photo courtesy of Dean Development Co.

The irregular lines of pool, decking and patio lend a natural look to this beautiful pool. Photo courtesy of Armstrong and Sharfman

Pool fences are protection against tragedy and are required by many local codes.
Photo courtesy of Hedrich-Blessing

This pool is heated by solar panels located on the roof of the house. Photo courtesy of Burke Solar Heaters

Many materials can be used around the pool. Natural rock is used for the coping of this irregular-shaped pool (left). The brick wall (above) protects vegetation from splash-out.

In-ground pools on small lots can cause space problems in providing for privacy. Here, the deck area leads into the house while a wooden fence increases pool privacy. Photo courtesy of National Swimming Pool Institute

Landscaping around the pool area can be simple and very functional. The pool receives full sun which helps heat the pool and reduce the energy costs.

This homeowner created small pond areas adjacent to the main swimming pool to grow natural water vegetation around the patio. Photo courtesy of Armstrong and Sharfman

Although the site is very small, this pool is made very attractive and comfortable through excellent landscape and pool design. Photo courtesy of Hedrich-Blessing

A well-designed pool will add beauty and value to a home for many years. Even on a poor day, the pool is attractive. Photo courtesy of California Redwood Association

Natural stone, vegetation, and exceptional design create this outstanding pool. This backyard "jungle" offers privacy and swimming in an attractive setting. Photo courtesy of Armstrong and Sharfman

This pool uses a series of rectangles to create interesting landscaping and seating areas. Photo courtesy of Armstrong and Sharfman

Although coping traditionally extends around the entire pool, outstanding designs can be created by bringing a higher wall to the pool edge. Photo courtesy of Armstrong and Sharfman

Underwater lights and a well-lighted poolside area allow safe night swimming (above left). Photo courtesy of Hedrich-Blessing

Poolside structures can be simple or as elaborate as this changing area-sauna. Photo courtesy of California Redwood Association

Large trees near the pool can create maintenance problems, but often the beauty overcomes this objection (right). Photo courtesy of National Swimming Pool Institute

Decking does not have to be expensive or elaborate to look good and be functional. A simple concrete deck and gravel offer an effective patio area. Photo courtesy of Fort Wayne Pools

The stone and wood structure at the end of this pool serves as a changing area and also houses the filter and pump equipment.

tors have eliminated this system in favor of gunite, some smaller pool builders who cannot afford the expensive gunite equipment still use it.

Either mortar set or interlocking masonry blocks can be used. The interlocking blocks require little know-how in stacking and could be used by the do-it-yourselfer. Like the poured concrete pool, the block system limits pool shape to either a rectangle or curved walls with very large radii.

To begin a block pool, the footing must be poured, usually about 12 inches wide and 18 to 24 inches deep. These footings need to be reinforced with steel bars for added strength. The floor can either be poured at the time the footings are installed or when the side walls are completed.

In-ground swimming pool construction is no job for the inexperienced, but with a knowledgeable owner-builder or contractor the work can be stunning. Photo courtesy of American Plywood Association

Ground pressure, strength of materials, and many other factors must be carefully considered for a good and long-lasting job. As can be seen from these photos, someone miscalculated, and ground pressure on the pool sides destroyed it.

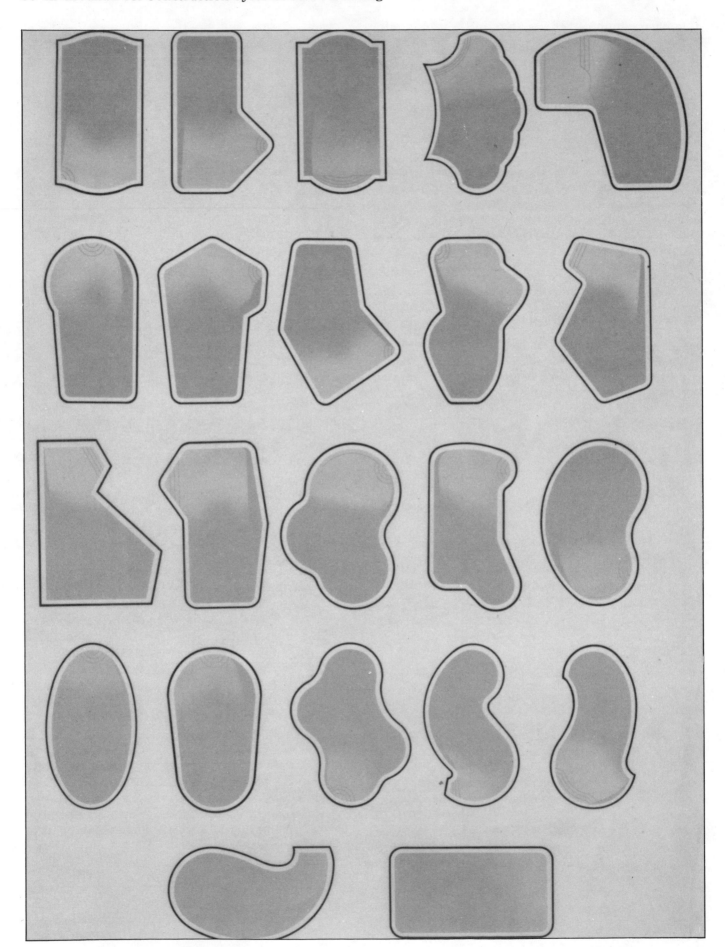

Heavy steel reinforcing bars are placed in the excavation and readied for the concrete mixture. Note blocks which keep steel off of the earth so that material can flow behind it.

If the walls are constructed first, it is wise to set the first row of block while the concrete is still workable; this affords a better seal. It also prevents the possibility of dirt falling on top of the footing and prevents leaks later on. As one course of block is completed, it is filled with grout to make the wall solid. Steel reinforcing also must be placed in these side walls as the designer recommends. Block side walls must be constructed very carefully. An uneven placement of block in the first or second row will be reflected throughout the entire wall.

Blocks should end about 8 inches or so from the top of the pool. Bend the steel reinforcing rods in the wall over, to be incorporated into the bond beam (the top of the wall which lips over to the ground). The bond beam must be poured next, and it must be wider than the pool wall.

As with poured concrete, careful arrangements must be made to leave openings for filter lines, skimmers, and drains.

Hand-Packed Concrete Hand-packed pools are a combination of poured concrete and gunite. The concrete is placed in the excavation without the aid of forms. A concrete mixer dumps the wet mix into the hole where it is hand applied to the walls and floor. Similar to gunite, it takes any shape made by the excavation.

The strength and durability of this system depend exclusively on the degree of expertise and care that the workmen use. For the do-it-yourselfer to attempt to use this system without any experience invites trouble, a lot of expense, and probably no swimming.

Common pool shapes available. Drawing courtesy of Wagner Aquatech Pools

Gunite The most popular concrete pool construction system today is gunite. The shape of your pool follows the final excavation shape. To do the job properly:

1. You must allow enough room for the equipment to get from the road to the excavation site.
2. You can have any shape pool you want.
3. The people completing the excavation must be competent.

Besides expertise, a gunite construction involves such equipment as a compressor, a cement mixer, and a hose and mixing nozzle. This array of expensive equipment keeps many smaller contractors from using gunite.

A gunite-constructed pool must first be carefully laid out on the ground and excavated with the walls shaped as specified. Then steel reinforcing is laid and interconnected to make the entire pool a monolithic structure.

With the steel properly adjusted, the gunite mixture of hydrated (very dry) cement and sand is shot from the hose nozzle until the steel is completely engulfed by the material. As the operator applies the mixture, an assistant watches that there are no pockets of unmixed sand or gravel buildup that could shorten the life or strength of the pool.

Once the gunite has been placed, a second crew immediately takes over and smooths out the walls and opens and cleans any drain or skimmer holes that might have been filled. There is less control over accidentally filling these lines in this process.

Fiberglass Pools Fiberglass pools acquired a poor reputation when they were first introduced because of leakage and poor reactions to certain pool chemicals. These problems have been corrected, and the fiberglass pool is now well worth considering.

There is a one-piece pool available that is delivered to your site and lowered into place by a crane. It comes with steps and coping, and requires little maintenance. Colorfast and resistant to black algae, the one-piece pool only comes in a few shapes and sizes.

A second type of fiberglass pool is made of wall panels. The prefab panels are bolted together at the site. The base of the panel is embedded in a footing of concrete. After the walls are secure, the concrete floor is poured and the stairs and coping are added. Far more flexible in shape than the one-piece unit, the paneled fiberglass pool requires higher maintenance due to the concrete floor.

Frames for Vinyl - Lined Pools This pool-building method is one of the most popular today. In some ways its construction is similar to above-ground pool systems. That is, a rigid wall is built and then the vinyl liner is added. Materials that can be used for the side

1.

2.

3.

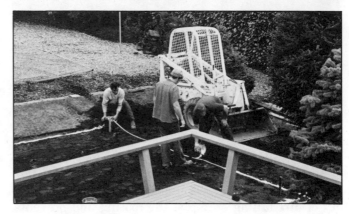

4.

walls of a vinyl-lined pool include aluminum, steel, wood, and concrete block. The same method for building the walls of a block concrete pool is used here. Although the walls do not have to be waterproofed, they must be smoothed so that the liner is not ripped or worn.

Unlike the above-ground pool, the excavation (for the metal or wood frames) of a vinyl-lined pool must be cut so that the panels can rest on evenly distributed firm earth. This is not easy. The metal or wood panels are delivered to the site and installed after the excavation is ready. They are bolted or welded together for a firm bond.

The excavation and installation of the panels must be exact so that the vinyl liner fits perfectly. An ill-fitting vinyl liner can cause serious problems, such as improper stretching, resulting in uneven wear and possible tears.

Steel panel units are designed to hold water without help from the ground around the pool and are good for problem sites such as hillsides or loose soil. They do, however, cost more. Aluminum and wood panels are far more popular because of their lower cost, lighter weight, and easier installation.

If you wish to undertake any part of building an in-ground pool with a vinyl liner, be sure you fully understand the instructions before any excavation is begun.

Finishing the Pool Interior Finishing off the

A pool with wood sidewalls and vinyl liner is an effective and simple system: (1) Sod is cut for removal; (2) Rolls of sod are taken for storage and later landscaping; (3) Measuring is done and stakes are placed; (4) Lime is spread between stakes to form guidelines for excavator; (5) Excavation begins; (6)

pool interior offers potential savings to those who wish to do it themselves. Many pools, of course, do not require finishing because of materials used. These include fiberglass and vinyl-lined pools.

Before tackling the pool finish, consult with your pool contractor or dealer. Often the cost of the finish is included in the base price of the pool package. What you could save by doing it yourself might not pay when you figure in the cost of materials, your labor, and the possibility of problems.

The three types of finishes commonly applied to concrete and to fiberglass pools that have a concrete base (walls will not require finishing) are tile, plaster, and paint.

Tile The beautiful, long-lasting finish of tile and its classic lines, combined with the many styles available, account for tile's additional expense. It also cleans well and is resistant to stains. This finishing material can run into thousands of dollars, depending upon the size of the pool.

In the typical residential pool today, tile is used from the waterline to the coping to give the pool a smooth, sleek look and prevent dirt buildup and water stains. It is used on the stringers of steps into the pool for the

5.

6.

7.

8.

Prefabricated plywood panels are placed; (7) Predrilled panels are joined to form retaining walls; (8) Panels are secured; (9) Sidewalls are stabilized with lumber bracing members; (10) Pool is completed and filled with water. Photos courtesy of American Plywood Association

same reasons. Tile comes in a variety of shapes and sizes: 2×2 inches up to 6×6 inches. Tiny mosaic tiles are probably cheapest.

These waterline tiles can be added by the homeowner. The major difficulties are proper tile alignment and careful application of grouting. For the cost involved it might be better to have a professional do the installation.

Plaster One of the most common and long-lasting pool finishes, plaster comes at a price most pool owners can afford. Do not try plastering the pool yourself. You paid a lot to get the pool built, and you don't want to waste that investment. Although the name is the same, swimming-pool plaster bears little resemblance to common house plaster. The problem with this material is that it sets rapidly. If it is not worked enough, it leaves a rough surface on the pool that looks poor and enhances algae growth; if it is worked too much, trowel burns will develop.

A good plaster job will last between ten and twenty years if the pool is maintained properly. If the pool is emptied without proper precautions, cracks will develop; if chemicals aren't properly applied and main-

9.

10.

tained, the plaster could etch.

Even though you are probably not doing this job yourself, you should know something about it. Plaster is composed of a granular media, white cement, water-

Although some in-ground pools can be constructed by the do-it-yourselfer, most cannot. If this is the only way you can make your in-ground pool work financially, be sure that the pool you want can be constructed by a novice. Here, a fiberglass-with-vinyl-liner pool is installed. Note carefully the number of hands needed to effectively place the liner. Photos courtesy of Fort Wayne Pools

proofing and hardening additives, and color if desired.

Usually a brown truing coat of ½- to ¾-inch is applied to the cleaned shell first. This establishes a bond and corrects any defects in the pool wall. Then one or two coats of hard thin white or color finish are applied as soon as possible. Now the finish must cure. It is best if this is done well before the pool is filled. Consult your pool builder before filling.

Paint Paint is the most inexpensive finish to apply to your pool, and is also one finish many homeowners can apply themselves. Some caution must be exercised before undertaking the job. Some paints are more difficult to apply than others, and you must be sure to cover every part of the surface area properly. If not, localized failures could develop and cause your pool to leak.

Before you begin painting, talk with your pool builder. He can advise you on the best way to proceed. He can recommend paints, check that your pool is ready for painting, and advise you on the best seasons and hours to do the job. Insects and dust can foul an outdoor paint job. Also, any surface to be painted must be absolutely clean before application. In the case of concrete pools, this means a good scrubbing with muriatic acid and then a thorough rinsing, allowing two to four hours for drying.

Similar to other paint jobs, a good roller or brush can be used. A roller allows you to apply the paint faster and usually gives a smoother finish. To estimate how much paint you will need, select a paint and see how much one gallon covers, then figure out how much more you will need for the rest of the pool. Buy paint thinner when you get the paint to speed cleanup.

There are a wide variety of paints available. One of the best is a chlorinated rubber base paint. Another good paint is epoxy enamel which gives a good finish that lasts three to five years.

Relatively inexpensive cement paint is one of the easiest paints for the homeowner to apply. Its chief drawback is that a new coating must be added every year to keep the surface smooth and looking good. If you don't want to do the pool draining and painting every year, it might be better to choose a more expen-

sive, but longer-lasting, paint.

Steel and aluminum pools should be prepared for paint by removing welded ridges. The material must be sandblasted and painted the same day. If it is left overnight, dew will begin the rusting process again.

Usually four to six coatings of paint are needed to ensure that the entire surface is covered. After the first season, you will usually see small areas or pinholes that you missed, because rusting will have begun. These should be sanded and repainted, and the paint should last another two to three years.

Above-Ground Pools

The above-ground swimming pool is an American invention that has spread worldwide since its introduction shortly after World War II. Although there were some very serious blunders and mishaps with early pool designs as manufacturers sought to rush these inexpensive pools to market, by the 1950s above-ground pools were firmly entrenched in the United States. Today, there are millions in place and the market has not yet shown signs of being saturated.

For the family which cannot or will not spend a lot of money on an in-ground pool but still wants to enjoy swimming, an above-ground pool is the logical answer. These units are relatively inexpensive. The pools can also be purchased as a package and a do-it-yourselfer can have his own pool ready for swimming after a weekend or two of work.

If properly maintained and cared for, the above-ground pool can last 10 years and perhaps longer. What's more, because it is not a permanent structure, it will not add to the tax bill as will an in-ground pool. If you decide to move, the pool can always be disassembled and shipped to your new residence. In short, the above-ground pool probably offers you the most "swimmability" per dollar investment.

There are, however, some drawbacks. Because the above-ground pool is not a permanent structure, it will not last as long as a good in-ground pool. Secondly, the above-ground pool can present some serious landscaping problems.

Size, Shape, and Depth

Above-ground pools were once limited in size and shape but today they come in a wide variety. The most popular shapes are round, oval, and rectangular units. The round ones vary from small 12-foot diameter pools with a 2,500 gallon capacity to a 28-foot diameter with an 18,300 gallon capacity. Oval pools can be as small as 18 by 12 feet to 40 by 16 feet. Rectangular pools follow similar dimension patterns.

You can buy above-ground pools with a uniform depth of either 3 or 4 feet, or you can obtain a pool that has a variable depth liner. This hopper is designed to give you a deeper pool for diving.

Above-Ground Pool Construction Systems

This chapter is not a do-it-yourself manual for an individual who wishes to construct an above-ground pool; instructions would vary from type to type and manufacturer to manufacturer. Reputable pool dealers always supply you with extensive information on how to put your pool together. A person who can use a

Above-ground pools offer a great value and use for the dollar invested. Although an above-ground pool will not last as long as a good in-ground pool, it has the added benefit of low initial cost and the pool can be erected by the do-it-yourselfer. Photo courtesy of Northeaster Chapter of The National Swimming Pool Institute

screwdriver, pliers, and other basic tools can put one of these pools together quickly if he or she follows directions.

Most above-ground pools have basically the same construction system. The walls are freestanding and are made of wood, aluminum, or steel. These wall units are fastened together and vertical supports are used to keep them in place. All pools use a vinyl liner which actually holds the water. Many units come with top railings or decking. Depending on how much money you want to spend, you can get very extensive decking, fencing, and a host of other extras.

The basic above-ground pool package will usually come with the equipment necessary for safe and sanitary operation. This includes a filtration system, automatic skimmer, test kit, and other items such as a vinyl liner repair kit.

Landscaping an above-ground pool can be difficult. One solution is to raise it and make it part of the house structure, similar to a patio. Photo courtesy of National Swimming Pool Institute

Purchasing Your Pool

Because many families are interested in a relatively inexpensive swimming pool, many dealers and other salespersons try to push whatever they are selling on price alone. You must exercise extreme caution when buying an above-ground pool. A good way to begin shopping for this type of pool is to write the NSPI for a list of above-ground pool dealers in your area.

Be cautious and watch out for newspaper ads showing a beautiful pool complete with everything for just a few hundred dollars. Looking at a picture of the pool, it would seem that you could fit your whole family and probably the entire neighborhood into it. Yet if you examine it closely, the ad might tell you that this is a 12- or 15-foot diameter pool.

The ads seek to whet your appetite with an inexpensive pool and then sell you a more expensive one once you have expressed dissatisfaction with the sale offer.

Companies such as these may be willing to give you a 20-year or lifetime guarantee on the pool and pool parts. Be aware that guarantees are only as good as the company behind them. A disreputable company will probably not be in business several years from now, and then you have a useless guarantee. Deal only with reputable pool dealers who have been in business in your community for a number of years, with many satisfied customers and references to prove it.

When purchasing an above-ground pool, determine what size, equipment, and extras will fill your family's needs. Do not decide on price alone: compare one company's product with others, and be sure you are comparing apples with apples. Make sure one package is offering the same quantity as well as quality as the other package. Does a ladder or diving board come with one pool and not the other? Look at the extras. Do you need them?

Above-ground pools come in a variety of shapes and sizes. The most popular are round, oval, and rectangular. Photos courtesy of Coleco Industries

Preparing the Site

Every type of above-ground pool will need its own individual site preparation. For the flat-bottomed pool you will need a site that is perfectly level. The ground underneath the pool must also be compacted if loose dirt is added. All sharp objects must be removed from underneath the pool. A sharp rock or piece of glass may puncture the liner immediately or may take several months to wear down the vinyl. In either case, it will greatly shorten the life of the liner. To prevent such rips and tears, some above-ground pool manufacturers specify a ground cover for the pool while others utilize sand as a base.

In any event, all vegetation must be removed either by pulling it out by the roots or by using a weed killer. Bermuda and St. Augustine grass can grow through some liners. When a weed killer or other chemical is used, it must be removed from the ground before laying the vinyl liner. Although the liner is impervious to natural chemicals in the ground, some man-made items can be very harmful to the liner.

Note on ground leveling: The ground upon which the pool sits must be absolutely level, not almost level. Any variation can cause a distortion in the pool wall, which could cause permanent damage to the free-standing wall and even void the guarantee you have on the pool.

When laying out the pool, you not only must consider how much to level for the actual pool, but also the space needed around the pool for other activities such as sunbathing and cleaning the pool with a hand

skimmer.

Once you mark the pool off, wait for a day or two. Look at the pool site from your house and walk around it. You should really like the location of your pool. The only way to do that is to live with the idea of the location for a while before installation. Although it is not impossible to move a pool, it is a waste of time, and the wall panels and the liner could get damaged in the process.

Although the directions within your pool package will undoubtedly specify it, you should know that the National Electrical Code requires that the pool pump and filters be grounded by a conductor in the cord. This does not include the metallic sides of the pool wall.

Build Your Own In-Ground Pool

As you have realized by now, pool building is not an easy task and in most cases it is a job better left to the professional pool builder. If curiosity or economics or extensive building experience has stimulated your interest to build an in-ground pool, this chapter, if read carefully, will allow you to understand what's involved. It is not meant as a manual for building an in-ground pool, but as an example of how to go about it. You must check with your building department and codes before you undertake such a project. There are things you can do yourself, and there are things for which you will be required to hire a licensed contractor. Often, you cannot do the plumbing or electrical work yourself. It all depends on local ordinances.

Options Available

As noted earlier, there are several pool construction methods. For the do-it-yourselfer, choices are more limited. From a cost standpoint, a concrete block with vinyl liner pool is best. In this system which will be fully detailed in this chapter, concrete blocks, which do not have to be waterproofed, act as sidewalls to hold back the earth and support the vinyl liner.

If easier construction outweighs cost considerations, you can construct an in-ground pool with one of the many fine pool packages on the market. These so-called packages are similar to above-ground pool kits in that they come with side walls of either wood, aluminum, steel, or fiberglass. Once the side walls are in place, a vinyl liner is installed to hold the water.

These kits are finely engineered for the do-it-yourselfer with limited skills and experience. For one price, the do-it-yourselfer can obtain everything he or she needs to build and successfully maintain the pool including filter, pump, and accessories. The disadvantage of the prepackage system is that costs are substantially higher than with a block and vinyl liner pool.

These kits come with comprehensive instructions to take you through every phase of planning, construction, and finishing. If you run into problems along the way, you can usually contact someone at the company who can help you rectify your problem.

Some in-ground pool systems should be shunned by the do-it-yourselfer altogether. A concrete block pool with a concrete bottom which is finished in plaster may not sound hard to build, but it is. Plaster pools have little in common with house plastering. Should you decide to build a pool of this type, do all the work yourself but bring in a tradesman for the plastering. It will be cheaper in the long run.

Other in-ground systems to stay away from if you plan to do the job yourself are gunite, or poured- and hand-packed concrete pools. Each of these systems requires either special equipment or technical knowledge beyond the scope of the do-it-yourselfer. These systems make outstanding pools, but they must be constructed by a professional.

Some pool systems use heavy steel as side walls. Where only bolting is necessary, the homeowner can probably do the job if the panel weight is not excessive. Unless you are an experienced welder, steel systems that require welding should be left to a qualified workman.

How to Plan a Do-It-Yourself Pool

As mentioned earlier, begin planning an in-ground pool by checking the local building and zoning and health departments to determine if a pool is allowed on your property. Most towns have booklets available on building codes and zoning regulations. These booklets should be studied carefully. In particular, look out for setback requirements. These regulations will not allow you (or your neighbor) to build a structure within a certain distance of the property line.

Your local codes may also help you decide if you can do the job yourself or wish to bring in outside help. Many codes require that all plumbing and electrical work be done by licensed tradesmen.

Should you decide to contract out most of the major work on the project, here are the people you would have to hire:

- architect or landscape architect
- excavator
- masonry contractor
- plumber
- electrician
- carpenter (if you want wood decks or other wood structures)
- landscaping contractor

Because swimming pool construction is such a multi-disciplined undertaking, many do-it-yourselfers will subcontract at least some of the work.

Concrete block pools are not the most versatile in shape, but they offer some variation. They can provide

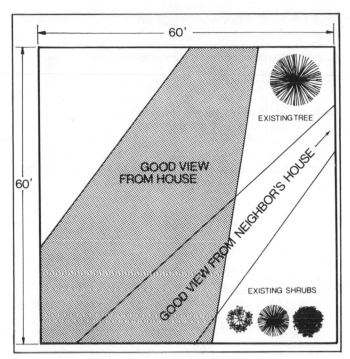

Lay out possible pool area on a larger sheet of graph paper. Make notes on all trees and shrubs to save, good views from your living room, views from neighbor's house which you wish to block, and anything else that might influence pool location.

years of swimming fun and a beautifully finished product. Typically, the concrete block pool has been either rectangular, teardrop, or kidney shape, but almost any shape can be constructed from concrete blocks as long as the radius of any curve in the pool is 10 feet or greater.

Rectangles of any size can be built. Many do-it-yourselfers find the 12 by 24 foot rectangular pool a project that they can handle and one that offers adequate swimming and splashing space. This size pool, of course, is slightly smaller than the average 15 by 30 foot pool which many contractors recommend. Other popular pool sizes include the 18 by 36 foot and the 20 by 40 foot pool. Rectangular pools are usually twice as long as they are wide. If you are thinking of selling your home at some time, it might be better to stick with a traditional configuration.

The easiest concrete block and vinyl liner pool to build is one with a flat bottom. The pool can be built with a standard depth of 4 feet, 6 feet, or more. Most do-it-yourselfers, however, like a pool with a shallow end and a deep end. The typical pool might range from a depth of 4 feet or less at the shallow end and 10 feet or more at the deep end.

Laying Out Your Pool You will need a plot plan before getting down to the actual design details of the pool. Look at the survey of your property which shows the property borders, exact house location, utility and sewerage systems, and all other obstructions on the property such as utility company right-of-ways.

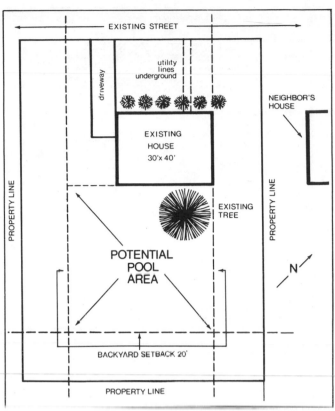

Draw a plot plan of your entire property on a piece of graph paper including all measurements, building locations, and any obstructions such as sewerage system or utility company right of ways. Then, after studying your building and zoning requirements, draw in all setbacks and other items that might restrict location of the pool.

Now draw your property to scale on a piece of paper, as in the illustration, making sure to include all zoning setbacks and requirements.

Now, on a new piece of graph paper draw the potential pool area to a larger scale. The larger you can draw this pool area, the more details you can add.

To get a feel for the pool area, take four stakes and actually mark it off in your yard to completely familiarize yourself with it.

Planning Your Own Pool It is virtually impossible to completely build a good, functional swimming pool yourself. In a concrete block and vinyl liner pool, obviously the liner will be purchased. Along with this, the filtration system, pool fittings, and other items will have to be purchased.

One of the first items in planning is to locate a reputable pool company with whom to do business. Before you get down to drawing the pool, you are going to have to know the specifications of all the parts. Do not settle for a catalog from the company; obtain the actual specification sheets.

Do not overbuild your swimming pool. If most of the labor will be done by you, you have to select a pool you can handle; a well-built 12 by 24 foot pool will be better than the olympic-size pool that is never completed.

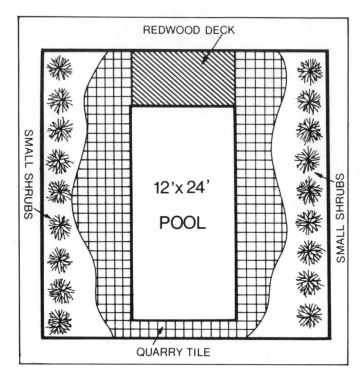

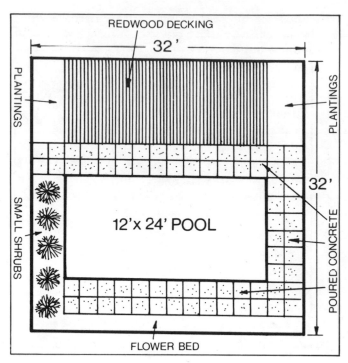

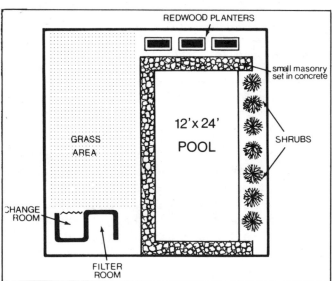

As can be seen from the illustrations, even when working with a specifically determined pool size and pool area, the potential for different layout is almost infinite. If your pool area contains any natural rock or interesting vegetation, the layout can be planned around them.

Some of the best pools featured in magazines are not necessarily the largest, but those having decks, patios, and landscaping tie-in to create a total look.

Although you must consider your family's needs when building a pool, the smaller you can make it, the less you will spend on materials and products at construction and the less you will spend on energy and chemicals.

The shape of the pool can also raise or lower costs. The rectangle is the least expensive to build. With concrete block you can also make a teardrop or kidney pool or any other shape for which a vinyl liner is made. These shapes will cost more than the rectangle.

If you are a first-time pool builder, another reason to choose a rectangle is that it minimizes construction difficulties. Once you select a vinyl liner, every effort

you make during design and construction will be aimed at making that liner fit exactly. It is hard enough to fit the liner to the rectangle, much less to the kidney or teardrop.

Building a Vinyl Liner Pool to Specification There are many vinyl liner manufacturers today. Some sell complete in-ground kits, but many will furnish you with just the liner and other desired accessory items. Once a supplier is selected, buy all accessories from that firm. A company that sells a substantial vinyl liner will also sell the proper filtration system to keep that volume of water in the pool clean and clear.

The typical vinyl liner ranges in thickness from .020-inch gauge to .030-inch gauge or $\frac{1}{20,000}$ of an inch to $\frac{1}{30,000}$ of an inch. There were some problems with seams in these liners when they were first introduced years ago, but these difficulties have been overcome.

Although liners can be purchased for a flat-bottom pool, most come with a deep end trough. Determining exact measurements for a rectangular pool is simpler than for other shapes.

Do Plot Plan First Once you have decided on a pool size, create a plot plan that includes your pool and pool area. This plot plan can be relatively simple. The intent is to determine if the pool is really an adequate size for you and your family and if you have enough room for other pool-related activities.

Once the plot plan is in final form, go out to your pool

area and stake out everything. Begin with the pool and add decks, patios, change houses, and other structures you plan to build.

Then live with your layout for a week or two. See if it is really convenient from the house. If small children are going to be swimming, can you keep an eye on the pool with your layout? Is there a safer layout, perhaps? If privacy is desired, does your fence layout furnish you with adequate privacy? How is the sunlight, shade, and access to the pool? In short, is this layout really what you want? Concrete block pools last a long time. Be sure of your needs and desires.

Designing the Pool

To illustrate how to design your own pool, the design of a small 12 by 24 foot pool will be detailed. The example has a shallow end of 4 feet and a trough or hopper makes the water 7 feet deep in the other end. To design your own pool, use the basics shown here.

About concrete block: a 4-foot high wall can be constructed with blocks 4 inches thick. A 5-foot high wall can be constructed with 6-inch blocks. A 7-foot wall can be built with blocks 9 inches thick. These are minimums. In the example cited here, the 4-foot high walls are being constructed with 8-inch block to give the pool more substance.

Your first drawing should reflect the inside dimensions of your pool (the dimensions of the vinyl liner). The outside dimensions should be the dimensions of your pool or liner plus two widths of 8-inch block. Add 24 inches on every wall—this will be the measurement of your excavation.

Next, draw an illustration reflecting the dimensions of the deep end hopper or trough. If you are building a flat-bottom pool, obviously you can eliminate this step.

Next, create a side view of the pool detailing the 24 foot side.

Finally, do a side view of the shortest side showing both the shallow end and the deep end.

Concrete Footings and Block Houses and other structures have substantial footings because of the

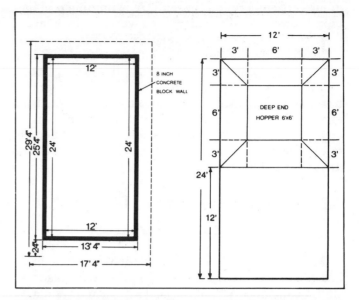

The first drawing details pool size on interior, exterior, and the exterior measurement plus 24 inches for each wall. This outer dimension is the size of the excavation that must be dug.

Now, design the deep end hopper. In this example, the hopper is 6×6 feet. In an actual pool, the hopper can vary in length and width.

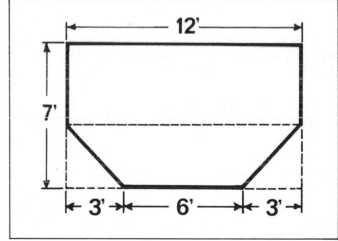

This diagram of the width of the pool at the deep end gives its dimensions.

The diagram, below left, is a view of the width of the pool at the shallow end, and the diagram, below right, is of the pool length, showing all measurements.

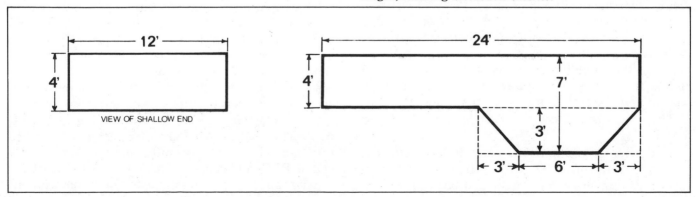

great vertical force on the wall. A swimming pool has only the weight of the block as a vertical force. Footings have very little effect against horizontal force.

Footings depend on soil conditions. If the soil is particularly loose or unstable, install a footing about 12 inches wide and 16 inches to 24 inches deep. For hard pan soil, little or no footing is needed. One structural engineer suggests that when the soil is stable, a footing about 6 inches deep should be poured to give the wall slight support, but mainly to level the area before laying block.

Designing the Pool's Support System

One of the biggest complaints do-it-yourselfers have had about the pools they build is the inadequacy or short operating cycles of the pool's filtration system. It is better to purchase a complete system, rather than individual components, to ensure getting parts that are compatible with each other. It makes little sense to buy a pump from one supplier, pipe from another, and the filter tank from a third.

If for some reason you must build a support system from scratch, you must first determine the exact volume of water in the pool. The formula for determining volume is length × width × average depth × 7.5.

Following are some facts about water: 1 cubic foot of fresh water weighs 62.4 pounds. One gallon of water weighs 8.3 pounds, and there are 7.5 gallons in one cubic foot of water.

To determine the volume of our example pool, we assume an average depth of 6 feet. Therefore: 12 feet × 24 feet × 6 feet × 7.5 (gallons per cubic foot) = 12,960 gals. of water.

All basic filtration systems contain five parts: the filter tank, pump, lint trap, recirculating pipe, and surface skimmer. Basically, every system operates the same way. The pump draws water from the swimming pool through the main drain, the surface skimmer, and the vacuum line, and forces it through the filtration media. The clean water then flows back into the pool via the recirculating pipe.

This system must be able to turn water every eight hours. This means in our example 12 by 24 foot pool with a 12,960 gallon capacity, the pool must filter that amount in eight hours, or 1,620 gallons per hour or 27 gallons per minute.

When the filter tank becomes filled with dirt and debris from the pool, the flow of water must be reversed and the system must be backwashed.

There are three basic filtration systems to choose from:

1. Conventional rapid flow sand filters are efficient and trouble-free. They filter the water with various size pieces of gravel and sand. They can effectively filter about 3 gallons of water per minute per square foot of surface area of the filter. For adequate backwashing, 12 to 15 gallons per square foot of surface area per minute are needed.

2. High rate sand filters have no gravel and operate on the principle of filtering the water in depth. That is, the debris is forced into the media. This system can filter up to 20 gallons or more per square foot of surface area per minute. Backwashing is accomplished at rates of about 20 gallons per minute per square foot of filter area.

3. Diatomaceous earth or D.E. filters are composed of a powder containing skeletons of tiny sea animals. This media can filter about 2.5 gallons of water per minute per square foot. But because the media is much more efficient than sand, less D.E. powder is needed. This reduces the size of the filter tank. Cleaning of the D.E. system is accomplished either by backwashing or by cleaning with a hose.

If we were trying to calculate the size of various filters for our example pool we would need a sand and gravel filter of approximately 9 square feet of surface area, a high rate sand filter of approximately 1.5 square feet, or a D.E. filter of approximately 11 square feet of surface area.

Swimming Pool Pumps Pumps can be located either to pull water from the pool and push it through the filter tank or pull it through the tank and push it back into the pool.

Pump performance is usually expressed in gallons per minute at a particular pressure known as "feet head." This means that when a pump is selected, it must be chosen not only with the amount of water to be pumped in mind, but also the pressure under which it must be pumped. This means the pump must have sufficient horsepower.

A great deal of care must be exercised when installing a pump. It should not be more than 2 feet above the pool water level and should, where possible, be at least 1 foot below it. The pump should be as close to the pool as possible and should never be placed more than 40 feet away from poolside.

Pipework and Layout Although it does not require a high degree of expertise, the pipework and fittings for a swimming pool must be properly laid out during design and construction for maximum efficiency. Various layouts of piping and equipment are possible. The idea is to prevent dead spots in the pool where water is left to stand and escape being filtered.

In the selection of piping for a swimming pool filtration system, there are four different types to choose from: galvanized iron, semiflexible polythene, rigid plastic PVC, and copper. Plastic pipe is the least expensive and offers resistance to corrosion. Not all

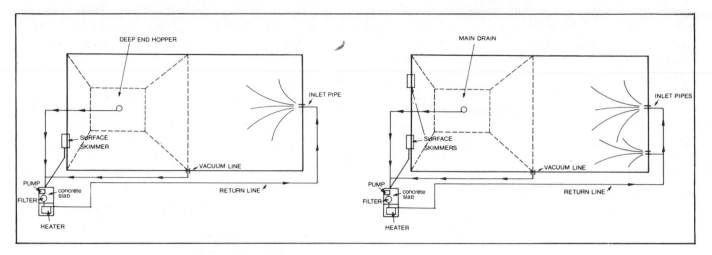

Two examples of filtration system layout. In the first there is one skimmer and one inlet pipe and one vacuum line. In the second there are two skimmers and two inlets. Placement of the skimmer must be determined by the prevailing winds around your pool and located downwind. That is, leaves, oil, and hair should be blown toward skimmer, not away.

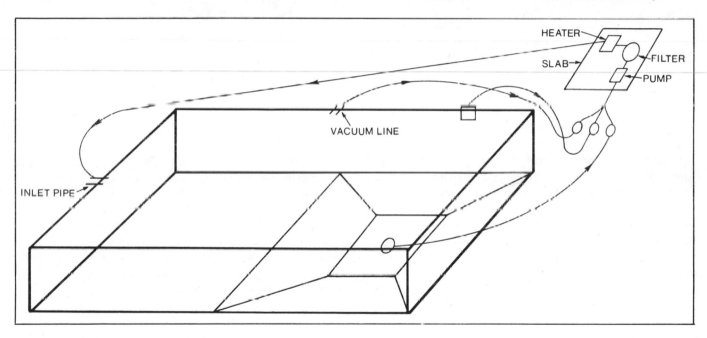

Side view of fittings placement. The main drain should be located in deepest part of pool trough. Vacuum fittings are at the surface, and the surface skimmer is a few inches under water.

building codes have yet accepted plastic pipe, so check before installation.

Do not use piping smaller than 1¼ inches and keep pipe runs as short as possible. Where runs are short and where there are not too many fittings, a 1¼-inch pipe can carry about 1,500 gallons per hour, a 1½-inch pipe about 2,500, and a 2-inch pipe about 5,000 gallons.

Consult with the company where you purchase the filtration system. If you are planning a rather extensive pool, bring in a specialist to help you set up your system. It costs money but it may save you considerable aggravation.

From your pool fittings specification sheets, you can determine the rough openings you will have to maintain when constructing the pool side walls. Mark the rough openings on the pipe layout and keep it handy when you are constructing the walls.

Pool Heaters Determining the size of a pool heater depends on the size of your pool, climate conditions, and the water temperature you desire. Because most heat is lost through the pool surface, you can use your surface square footage to calculate heat loss and thus the heater size. In our example pool, we have 288 square feet of surface area. Generally speaking, you can figure on losing about 15 BTU's of heat per square foot of surface area per hour for every degree that the

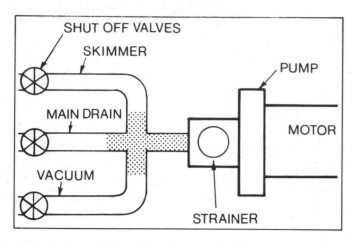

Typical union of three lines from swimming pool to pump.

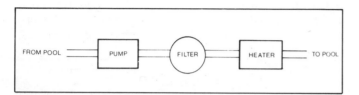

Typical hookup of heater into swimming pool system. The heater does not have to be purchased at the time the pool is installed if a coupling is added for later heater hookup.

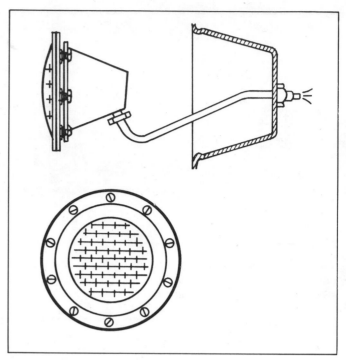

Typical wet-niche lights for pools. Most codes specify that these units must be placed at least 18 inches below the surface of the water.

pool water is above air temperature. To determine the size of the heater needed for your pool, multiply the square footage, 288, by the 15 BTU heat loss. Therefore, 288 × 15 = 4,320. Then you multiply 4,320 by the number of degrees you wish to keep the pool water above air temperature. If you want the pool water 10 degrees above air temperature, 4,320 × 10 = 43,200. A heater which will produce 43,200 BTU's of heat per

hour is needed to maintain pool temperature 10 degrees above air temperature. For larger pools, the demand would be much greater. Some pool builders recommend that you use a heater which is oversized for your pool. That is, a unit which produces far more BTU's than you need. If you use your pool only on weekends, you can shut the heater off on Sunday and leave it off until Friday. Then you can switch it on, and because the heater is oversized, it heats the pool more quickly than a heater sized exactly for your pool. Although the heater initially costs a little more, energy savings may more than make up the extra cost.

Electrical Wiring for the Pool Your local building code will be the determining factor in how electrical wiring is installed in and around pools. The National Spa and Pool Institute also has a pamphlet available entitled "Swimming Pool Wiring."

Briefly, all metallic parts within a specific distance of the pool must be grounded.

Underwater lights are also covered by the code. The National Electrical Code specified several acceptable systems. One system is a 110-volt lighting fixture with built-in ground detection devices that can sense a break in the connection. Another system is a low-voltage (12-volt) unit which uses high-wattage bulbs.

According to the NEC, the inside bottom of junction boxes for 110-volt systems must be mounted 8 inches above water or deck level and 4 feet away from the pool. Metallic niches for lights are usually a must and should be placed 18 inches below the surface of the pool.

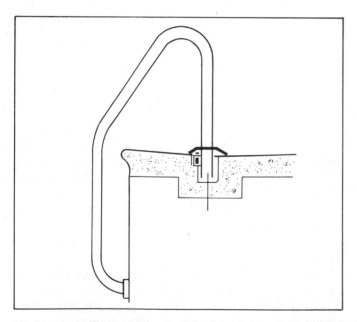

Ladder installation in a vinyl-lined pool must be planned during design. The grab bar is anchored in the deck area with concrete. The part below waterline rests against the liner.

Today, wet-niche lights are used almost exclusively. Dry-niche lights can be dangerous if the lens is accidently broken.

Pool Ladders and Diving Boards Designing in pool ladders and diving boards for vinyl liner pools is simply a matter of marking off the area around the pool to anchor the units. These accessories are never anchored through the vinyl liner.

If a full ladder is not mandatory, grab bars are a less expensive substitute. Stainless steel and chrome-plated units are usually used.

Planning the Pool Coping The coping is the lip of the pool and supplies a transition from the water to the deck. It also acts as a hand grab for swimmers and prevents splash-out from reentering the pool. The coping can be of any water-resistant, nonskid substance from paving stone to coping stone to redwood boards. The only requirement is that it slope away from the pool.

Construction of the Pool

Once all design and layout considerations are complete and you have received necessary approvals from local building and zoning departments, you can begin construction.

Excavation is first. As mentioned previously, the actual excavation should be approximately 24 inches larger than the pool size. This gives you room to build the block wall and install any fittings with relative ease.

Therefore, in our sample, the 12 × 24 foot pool must actually be laid out approximately 16 to 17 feet × 28 to 29 feet.

The layout for the excavation can be easily completed by carrying out the steps in the following illustrations.

Level Excavation Before Digging The top of the excavation will normally be surrounded by decks, patios, or walk area; therefore, it should be as level as possible. The pool, of course, can be installed on almost any grade. The only restriction is that the pool itself must be level and rest on solid earth.

If the site has a steep slope, it is best to set the narrow side of the pool parallel with the slope to cut down somewhat on the grade change from one side of the pool to the other. Another alternative for a steep slope is to cut back into the earth on the high side for 10 feet or so to help level the site.

Place a mark on the highest stake to determine the top surface of your pool. A mark must be placed on the other three stakes, level with the first mark, to establish the swimming pool level.

Try to rent a transit level for this operation. If a transit or dummy level is not available, the pool top can still be determined. Secure a mason's string to the

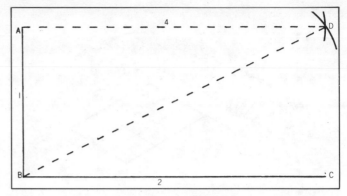

Corner A, which should be the highest corner of the pool, should be laid out first. It can be determined by eye or by measurement—it goes where you want it to. Drive a stake in the ground. Measure off one side of the pool exactly and drive another stake in the ground. We have now determined stake A, stake B, and Side 1, when we tie a string between A and B. Use Stake B as the center point of a circle. Measure off the distance of Side 2 on a string as in the illustration above. Tie a nail to the other end and with the string tight, scribe an arch in the ground at approximately right angles to stake B. Next calculate the diagonal line AC (use the formula $AB^2 + BC^2 = AC^2$). Measure a line equal to the diagonal line. Tie it to stake A, pull it taut, and scribe another arch in the ground at approximately the same area as previously. Where the arches intersect, stake C should be driven.

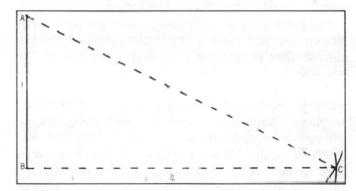

Repeat this step, only this time—measure off side 4. Use Stake A as the center and scribe an arch at approximately right angles to stake A. Then use the diagonal line again with stake B as the center and scribe another arch to intersect it. Where the archs intersect, stake D can be driven.

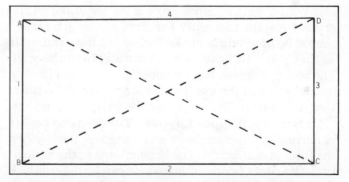

Then connect stake D and stake C with a string, and the excavation is laid out. You will have to repeat this process to obtain the final pool layout later.

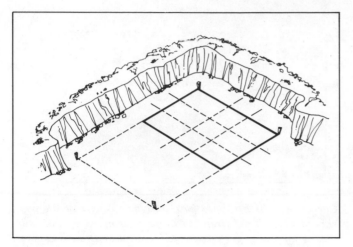

Create three sets of guide marks around the perimeter of the pool. Where they intersect is the position of the pool hopper. Indicate these guide marks well so that the excavator can line his shovel up with them as he digs.

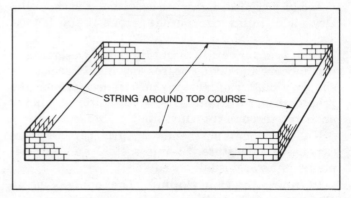

Build blocks at corners first. Lay three or four courses at each angle, then step blocks up 3 or 4 courses. Make sure that corners are proper dimensions and that blocks are square and level. Once these corners are properly installed, the rest of the job is easy. Attach a string to the top course, as in the illustration. As you build the walls, the outside of the blocks should just touch the string.

first stake at the level you desire. It is best to also mark this stake with a crayon at the level mark in case the string slips later.

Place a line-level midway along the string and adjust the position of the string on the second stake until it is level. Mark the stake well and repeat the operation until all stakes have a level mark.

Once the level is determined, use either chalk powder or flour and make a line on the ground under the string. This is to outline the hole to be dug by the excavator.

Next to a hand-dug hole, a backhoe or Grandall disturbs the ground the least. The hole can now be dug to the greatest uniform depth. In the case of our example pool, we would want to dig the excavation to 4 feet.

Work with the excavator. Fashion your own measuring stake out of a long 1 × 2 inch board. Mark off 4 feet on it. As the excavator digs, push the stick in the hole. When the line on the stick lines up with the string previously leveled, the excavator will know the hole is deep enough in that section.

Once this section of the excavation is completed, the exact layout of the pool must be determined. With the excavation well leveled, drive a corner stake in the ground—again to signify the first corner. The stake should be approximately 24 inches out from the walls so that you will have room to work behind the wall. The pool dimension you are seeking to lay out is for the inside wall and the exact dimension of the vinyl liner. Use the same procedure as for the excavation layout.

Determine Hopper Layout The deep end hopper is normally a rectangle in a rectangular pool. When the final layout for the pool is completed in the excavation, the exact hopper dimensions can be determined. Depending on your hopper size and location, create three sets of guide marks around the perimeter of the pool as shown in the illustration.

Fashion another longer stick from a 1 × 2 and mark off the depth of the hopper on the stick. Most vinyl liner manufacturers specify either 2 or 3 inches of sand be placed under the liner. If this is the case with your liner, mark off the depth of the hopper plus 2 or 3 inches on the stick.

Accuracy is the key to a professionally installed vinyl liner pool. This requirement begins with the excavation and is vital in the digging of the deep end hopper. As indicated in your drawings, the hopper must be excavated to a certain depth and then the walls must be sloped, generally by hand.

When the excavation is in relatively good shape, the main drain should be located in the deepest end of the pool. It can be set either in the center or toward one side near the pump.

The main drainpipe must be installed before any work is started on concrete block walls. The pipe must run from the main drain pot across the pool floor, under a few inches of dirt or sand, under the wall, and to the filtration area.

Many pool builders add a hydrostatic relief valve to allow groundwater to enter the pool when pressure is great enough. This prevents the pool from "floating." Pool builders have differing opinions on whether to add a hydrostatic relief valve to a vinyl-lined pool. They say the valve should always be added to other types of pools, but for vinyl-lined pools, some prefer to have the pool float somewhat, rather than risk a particle of sand clogging the mechanism and then emptying the pool. The addition of a hydrostatic relief valve is up to you.

Laying the Pool Footing The footing does not have to be extensive if the ground is firm. If soil conditions dictate, and you might not know conditions until you actually excavate, add a footing.

Dig a trench along the perimeter of the pool directly

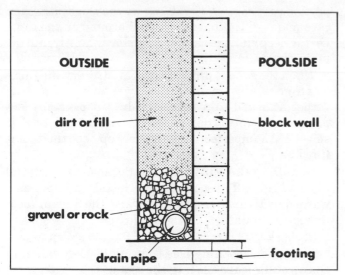

Drainage at the foot of the wall will prevent a buildup of hydrostatic pressure against the walls. Place a drainpipe of several inches diameter around the entire perimeter of the pool wall. The pipe should slope slightly and drain either into a dry well or to a low point on your site. Add between 12 and 16 inches of gravel or small rock on top of the pipe for drainage. Many do-it-yourselfers add a manhole near the pool drainage to see how high the water level is around pool wall. This can be no more than an 8-inch clay pipe. By shining a flashlight into it, you can determine water level. If water gets particularly high, rent a pump and pump water out through your manhole.

under where the block will be laid. Do not add a form for the footing on top of the soil, otherwise the pool wall will be too high. An accurately dug trench can also act as the form for the footing. If your soil is loose, consider the addition of several steel reinforcing rods throughout the footing to tie it in together. Whether you work off a footing or solid, packed earth, the area must be level before beginning block work.

Building the Swimming Pool Side Walls Blocks should be laid at corners first, to make the rest of the job easier. Build out three or four courses of blocks, then build up three or four courses, stepping the blocks as you go.

You can purchase a ready-mix concrete for the masonry work, or you can mix your own. For ordinary service, mix one part masonry cement to 2.5 or 3 parts mortar sand. In areas where severe frosts are possible, mix one part masonry cement and one part portland cement to 4.5 or 6 parts masonry sand. When possible, rent a mixer to save time. It is tedious, backbreaking work to mix any volume of masonry by hand.

When constructing the walls, scrape off all excess mortar from the blocks, preventing the material from falling into the excavation. Often the masonry cement hardens into sharp little rocks which could later damage the liner.

As you build the walls, leave open spaces for the installation of lights, skimmers, inlet line, and other

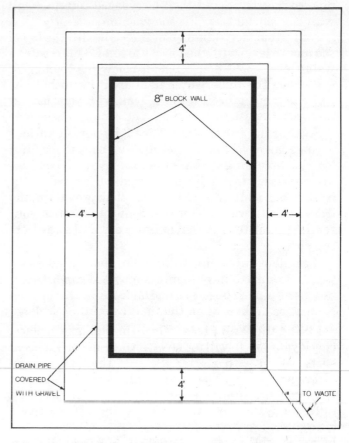

Where severe drainage problems exist, place drainpipe around pool as previously indicated. Then four feet out from pool in a perimeter around the pool, dig down to the depth of the pool wall and install a similar drainage system. A drain system several feet from the pool is particularly beneficial if the pool is located near a hill, which of course would drain rainwater in the direction of your pool.

accessories. Check your specification sheets and make all rough openings the precise size.

Depending on the quality of the job you do, you won't have to add anything else to the wall before the liner. The walls, however, must be smooth with no sharp points. All joints must be flush and smooth. Cove each corner to a minimum of a 2-inch radius with mortar mix.

Drainage Depending on what you found after excavation, you might have to add some drainage to the swimming pool. In a typical pool wall, there will be hydrostatic pressure on the outside of the wall. This should be more than offset by the pressure from inside the filled pool.

To prevent a large buildup of pressure on the outside, you can add a drain near the bottom of the wall.

Connecting Pool Fittings The swimming pool fittings must be connected as per the instructions provided with the units you purchase. The inlet spreaders are screwed to a connector which is then passed through the wall. A bend and polythene pipe coupling is connected to the end which is outside the pool. The pipe connector should then be wedged into the wall with the mortar mix. Fit the vacuum similarly.

Set the surface skimmer in the wall with the top of the mouth level with the top of the liner. This creates a water level about 4 or 5 inches below the coping.

Remove the underwater light from its niche. The niche is then embedded in the wall with your mortar mix with the fitting to connect the conduit at the top.

Setting the Pipework The piping for the various fittings can now be connected and run back to the filter location according to your pipework layout. If trenches are necessary to reach the filter, dig them below the frost line in your area. Once connected, provide piping from filter to waste. This can connect either to your septic system, town sewer, or into a dry well away from the pool.

If possible, run piping behind the concrete block side walls. Be sure to have firmly compacted earth underneath the pipe. If pipes are laid on loose earth, they can be bent or broken when the final backfilling is done.

Fixing the Wall Plate Once the piping is in place, check your block wall for level. If there are any uneven spots, fill in with mortar. Be sure the wall is level before proceeding. Then add a wall plate. The supplier from whom you purchase the vinyl liner may have a different system for attaching the liner. If not, select straight 2×8s or a timber the same width as your blocks. Nail the wall plate flat on the blocks. It is not designed to take much pressure so the plate can be nailed (with masonry nails) into the block about 2 feet on center.

The vinyl liner can be attached to this plate in a number of ways. Some do-it-yourselfers fold the liner over the plate and use a 1×2 to secure the liner. Others simply staple the liner to the plate or buy plastic stripping specifically designed for this purpose. The point is, this plate and the liner do not support water; the wall merely holds the liner in place, and the water sits in the liner.

Later, after the liner is attached, this timber plate can be covered with a coping material of your choice.

Placement of Sand The look of the inside of the pool will depend on how well the sand is placed. The sand, of course, acts as a cushion between liner and earth. To get maximum evenness, wash the sand before dumping on the pool bottom. Check directions furnished with the liner for how many inches of sand you need. A pencil can be marked off at 2 or 3 inches and used to measure the thickness of the sand as it is applied.

Dump sand and rake, checking the depth constantly. Use a garden roller or tamper to compact the sand. Be sure all sand is firmly compacted. To get the slopes even, attach a rope to the roller and invite a few friends over to help you pull it up and down the slopes.

Once the sand is compacted do not walk on it. Be particularly careful of walking up the slope after sand is compacted. Use boards to walk around on the sand. On the deep end, the sand should slope slightly into the main drain.

When the sand is properly prepared, remove all articles from the pool interior. Use a wet towel or a piece of carpet attached to a rope and drag it over any imperfections until the entire interior of the pool is smooth. An imperfection will show up once the pool is filled.

Installing the Vinyl Liner Because the material tends to get stiff in cool weather, install the liner on a warm day. If this is impossible, warm the liner at room temperature until it is highly flexible.

Recheck the bottom of the pool for any sharp stones, branches, or anything else that might have fallen in since you finished placing the sand.

Take liner and box to poolside and make sure the deep end portion is positioned for the deep end. Unfold the liner with help from your family or friends. Have one person take each corner of the liner and carefully move to the four corners of the pool. Most suppliers mark the corners.

Once the liner is suspended over the excavation, begin pushing it in so it fits each corner snugly. Temporarily fix the liner at the timber plate with weights. You can use quite a bit of force to pull the liner into place.

Air will be trapped underneath the liner. Use a vacuum cleaner to draw the air out. In 15 or 20 minutes the air will be drawn out, and the liner will be flush against the walls and on the bottom. Use a broom or pool brush from outside the pool, and smooth out any wrinkles. The fit must be exact before water is added.

The hole should be cut for the main drain at this time. Begin filling the pool with water from a garden hose. Even if you intend to fill the pool with water from a high pressure source, begin with a garden hose so no indentation is left on the sand.

As the pool is filled, brush out all wrinkles. Tape all areas where the liner will have to be cut for fittings. No openings should be cut for fittings until the water level approaches the fitting. If the liner is cut too soon, it could stretch and tear. Follow all directions included with the vinyl liner package for fitting.

Once the water level approaches the fittings, the liner can be cut with a sharp knife or razor blade. The wall fitting should already be in place, and you can attach any front fittings necessary.

Backfilling should be a continuous process as the pool is filled. When the pool is full, the backfilling should be complete. Do not lay a concrete deck until the backfill is settled. If using a machine for this work, do not allow any large rocks to come in contact with the wall.

Ladders and other accessory items should come with anchors. The ladder should be cemented into the ground according to instructions. The ladder should be level and plumb. Do not disturb it until the cement has cured.

When the pool is filled, you can begin operating the filtration system. Because there are so many different systems, consult your manufacturer's manual for proper start-up and maintenance.

Around the Pool

The do-it-yourselfer can save considerable money on decks, sunning areas, and other poolside areas. Many of these areas are optional while others, although not included in the swimming pool plan, are almost imperative. Outdoor furniture is one such case. Because these options may be purchased, custom-made, or built by the homeowner, prices can vary drastically.

When decks are planned, it is not only how the work is done that affects the price, but also the materials used. There is a tremendous choice. If you want an expensive, redwood decking, you can reduce costs by doing much of the carpentry work yourself. Some kits for decking are on the market for the do-it-yourselfer. On the other hand, a cheaper form of decking may suffice, and the time saved installing the deck can be turned into time used to create special sunning platforms, benches, or whatever else the family desires.

Money saving can also mean watching for items that serve two purposes. Can a card table be instantly converted into a family picnic table? Can a stationary bench have a storage area underneath? Can you house the filter system in a shower room or cabana? Custom creating your own poolside extras is only limited by imagination.

Decks

Take your pick. Decks may be large, small, evenly spaced around a pool, irregularly patterned, and made of wood, rocks, flagstone, patio blocks, bricks, indoor-outdoor carpeting, or aluminum. There's a variety of colors as well as textures. You cannot estimate the cost until you've decided upon the deck size, materials, and who will do the work. Materials, too, vary in cost from one section of the country to another. In choosing your deck, you also have the choice of whether you wish to eliminate the coping and have the decking right up against the pool. You may find that it integrates the pool more dramatically with the immediate surroundings.

Whatever decking materials you choose and how you plan to install them, the deck should always serve the two purposes for which it was intended. It should act as a safe walkway and lounging area and at the same time set off your pool as a picture frame does a picture. There are two rules for decking materials. The surface, when wet, should be nonslippery, and the material should be relatively cool underfoot, even on hot days.

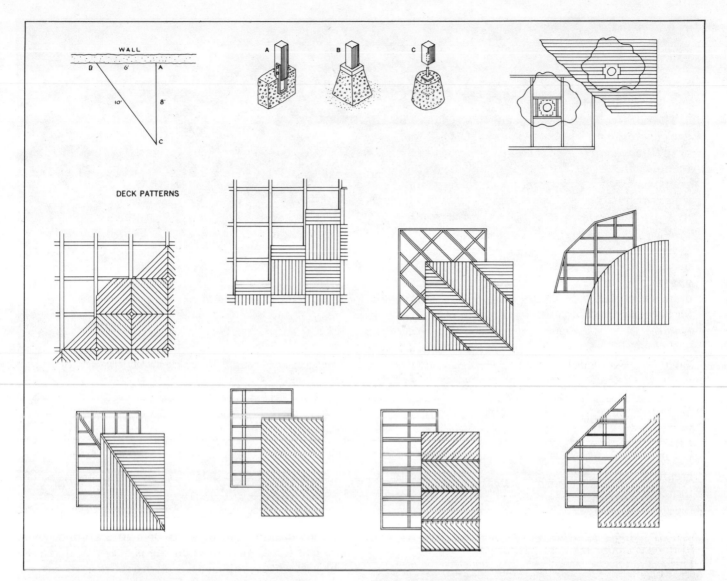

Wood decking supported by footings (A, B, or C), offers flexibility in planning the area around a pool. Offered are a variety of designs a do-it-yourselfer can use for building decks. Drawings courtesy of California Redwood Association

For problem areas—too much sun, too little space, overhanging trees, hillside situations, or special climate conditions—you should be aware that certain textures, colors, and materials can go a long way in answering your needs.

Decking Materials The most inexpensive decking in and around the pool is a grass which has a pleasant texture underfoot. Its disadvantage is that grass clippings and dirt can find their way into the pool from the soles of swimmers' feet. Another difficulty is splash-out. Chlorine will kill the vegetation and cause a mud problem. Grass can be a good solution for the part of the pool area that does not get a lot of water traffic.

Modular or monolithic pavement block is relatively inexpensive and can make a nice decking. It is cool underfoot and can be installed by the homeowner. Another inexpensive possibility is a broomed concrete. This decking is created as is any concrete slab, but it is finished with a stiff broom rather than floats. This affords interesting patterns on the surface and creates a durable, nonskid surface. Slab materials, however, sometimes crack, particularly in colder climates. A way to get around this is to score the surface in any pattern you like by using an electric saw with a carbide blade. If any surface cracking occurs, it will follow the scoring and not be noticeable.

One of the best ways to furnish a good-looking inexpensive decking is to sprinkle pebbles around your pool area. Strips of redwood can be integrated with the pebbles to create interesting patterns. This material can either be left permanently or removed when other more expensive decking and landscaping plans are executed.

If your ground is firm, you can usually add brick, flagstone, or quarry tile directly on the ground. If the soil is unstable, it might be necessary to lay a slab before applying the decking material.

Brick is a durable, attractive decking material. Photo courtesy of National Swimming Pool Institute

Flowers in easily made wooden planters add a homey, bright touch to decks around pools, especially for the do-it-yourself gardener. Photo courtesy of California Redwood Association

Wood decking can be quite beautiful around pools and can function well when the pool is out of grade. The best woods for pool decking are redwood, cedar, or any self-preserving wood. These woods require very little maintenance.

Outdoor Furniture

You may wish to purchase inexpensive folding furniture your first year to see exactly what you will need and where you want to place it. You may see that comfortable chairs are far more popular with your family than are reclining chaise lounges. Will you need a sun umbrella? Will several snack tables be of better use than an outdoor eating table?

Prices vary for outdoor furniture. Be sure it is durable, water resistant and fade resistant, and will comfortably fill the needs of your family. It will need to be stored during the winter months.

Look for ways to use any stationary furniture for storage. It is invaluable around a pool for storing games, air mattresses, toys, and extra towels. Other ideas for multiple-purpose items may occur to you as you use your pool.

Outside lighting is a plus for many pools. Here, 150-watt PAR-38 floodlamps are mounted on poles, with one lamp for every 45 square feet of surface to be lighted. Poles should be placed at either side of the pool, about 10 feet from the deepest end. Circling the pool are small lanterns with low-wattage bulbs which serve as a decorative accent and heighten the festive aura of the pool. Photo courtesy of the American Lighting Institute

Barbecue and Eating Areas

Again, what you do and how you do it will determine the price. A small, portable barbecue, may suit your needs. If you have planned for an eating area, you can build the barbecue yourself at your leisure.

Choosing a Location The barbecue is best situated near the house, close to fuel, food, and utensils. In fact, many excellent barbecues have been built against the outer wall of a house, utilizing the house chimney stack. Avoid putting the barbecue and eating area next to the pool or in the pool traffic pattern. Food can also attract insects, unwelcome pool guests at any time. To ensure against these problems, screenings, plantings, or fencing can separate your eating area from the pool. Refuse disposal should be handy. Arrangements for eating areas can include a simple picnic table and portable barbecue or can mean a masonry barbecue and patio area complete with refrigerator and sink. Another important concern will be the view of the pool from the eating area—light on the water on a warm summer evening enhances outdoor eating pleasure.

Getting Started Outdoors You can either hire a competent mason or, if you have a knack for outdoor tasks, you can wield the trowel yourself. The first problem in either case is that of a proper foundation so that the structure will not settle or sag. Many builders prefer to excavate below the frost line, pouring a 6-inch concrete foundation. If your pool will be concrete also, you can have the barbecue and pool foundations poured at the same time to save money. Many excellent barbecues, however, are supported on the floating slab principle. A shallow excavation is made, and a concrete slab is poured, reinforced with 6×6 inch wire road mesh. Depending on the size of the barbecue, the slab should be from 4 to 6 inches thick and should extend at least 4 inches outside the barbecue boundaries.

Installing Equipment For amateur installations, there is sometimes the temptation to improvise metal features. You might make a grill from parallel steel rods, cemented tightly in place. But the rods will soon warp or sag; expansion loosens the masonry bond. Try purchasing a unit manufactured specifically for the purpose by a reputable manufacturer. Follow manufacturer's instructions and allow for expansion.

No single unit is likely to satisfy all the desires of the open-fire chef, so plan your equipment requirements with care. Dutch ovens, powered- or hand-operated spits, adjustable fire levels, and cleanout doors are among items to consider.

A chimney is sometimes necessary. If you will be burning only charcoal, walls around the metal units are sufficient. However, if either wood or coal might be used, the barbecue should have a chimney.

Outside Light and Heat

You may choose either gas lighting, if permitted, or electric bulbs that do not attract insects. This is not a do-it-yourself job. Special grounded wiring is used in and around pool areas. It should conform to the electrical code and laws in your vicinity. Ask your contractor or architect where and if you should install outdoor lighting for your family's needs.

For night entertaining or cool months, you might

Fences mean more pool safety and privacy. Wood is one of the best materials for the do-it-yourselfer because it is relatively inexpensive, lightweight, and workable. The various styles of fences shown here can be easily handled by the do-it-yourselfer. Drawings courtesy of California Redwood Association

Potted plants and vegetation in planters are excellent landscaping materials around the pool. The advantage to this design is its adaptability—when you wish to change the arrangement or add to it, just move the plants. Photo courtesy of California Redwood Association

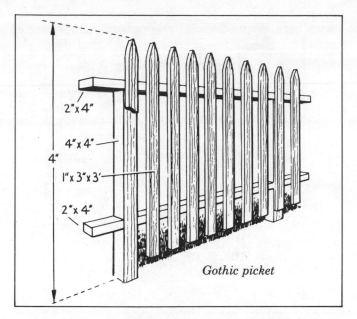

2" x 4"

4" x 4"

1" x 3" x 3'

2" x 4"

4"

Gothic picket

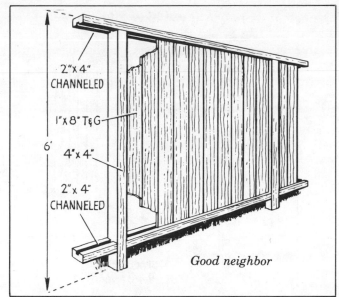

2" x 4"
CHANNELED

1" x 8" T&G

4" x 4"

2" x 4"
CHANNELED

6'

Good neighbor

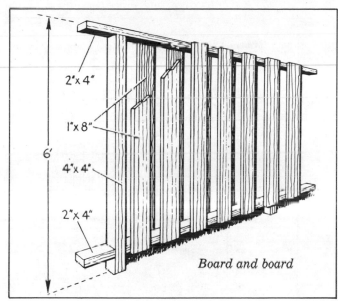

2" x 4"

1" x 8"

4" x 4"

2" x 4"

6'

Board and board

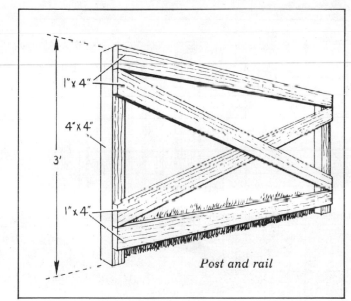

1" x 4"

4" x 4"

1" x 4"

3'

Post and rail

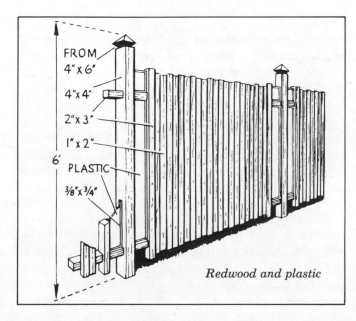

FROM
4" x 6"

4" x 4"

2" x 3"

1" x 2"

PLASTIC

⅜" x ¾"

6'

Redwood and plastic

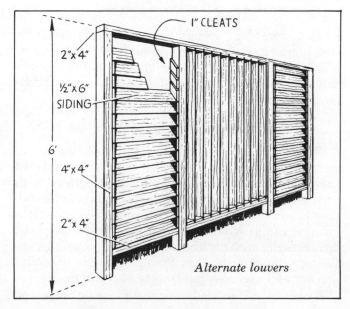

1" CLEATS

2" x 4"

½" x 6"
SIDING

4" x 4"

2" x 4"

6'

Alternate louvers

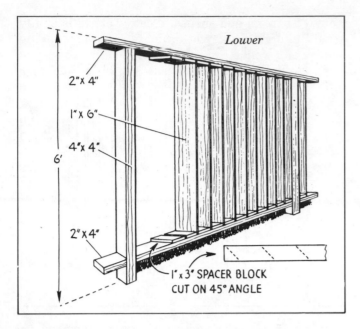

Louver

2"x 4"
1"x 6"
4"x 4"
6'
2"x 4"
1"x 3" SPACER BLOCK
CUT ON 45° ANGLE

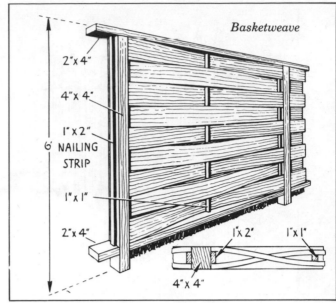

Basketweave

2"x 4"
4"x 4"
1"x 2"
NAILING
STRIP
6'
1"x 1"
2"x 4"
1"x 2"
1"x 1"
4"x 4"

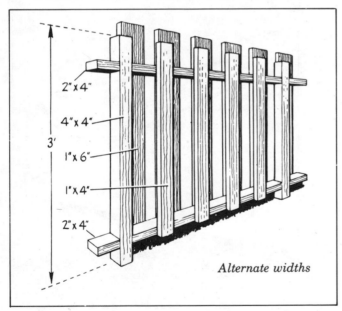

2"x 4"
4"x 4"
3'
1"x 6"
1"x 4"
2"x 4"
Alternate widths

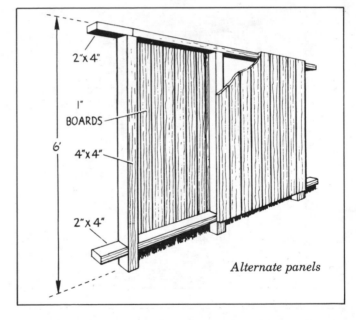

2"x 4"
1"
BOARDS
6'
4"x 4"
2"x 4"
Alternate panels

want to consider poolside heating arrangements. A well-placed electric heater may answer your needs, or a specially built fireplace or brazier might be more suitable. You may even be able to use your barbecue for this purpose.

A Comforting View

Whether you see your pool from the house or are sitting on the poolside facing out, your pool should give the impression of being completely integrated with your land and your home. Pleasant landscaping can mean shelter from winds, or a lovely tree at the right location can provide shade at the hottest time of the day. Fencing, although required by law in most localities for the protection of young children, can offer privacy and eye-catching beauty at the same time.

There is no limit to how much money or time you can spend on these items. Landscaping can be planned and begun at the time of the pool's construction, but you may complete the job at any time. Fencing or sheltering your pool (provided you comply with the law in your locality) can be done the same way.

Fences Like decking, fences come in a variety of shapes, textures, materials, colors, and prices. You can buy kits, do it yourself from scratch, or have it done for you. There is no right or wrong fence, but a fence can enhance or detract from a particular poolside area. Your own judgment and advice from a landscape architect or builder will help determine what would be most suitable visually, serve as protection from winds and sun, and offer privacy.

Fences do not have to be straight; they come free-form, circular, high, low, or just about any design imaginable. Fences may be interspersed with plantings, and in many cases the effect is quite handsome. Fencing materials may be of wood, wire, mason blocks, brick, or any number of other variations. They keep out toddlers, may be removable, and even come with special safety gates.

Sheltered Pools Fencing, fiberglass panels, plantings, or trellises can shelter a pool. The position of a pool in relation to your house can protect a pool. The idea is to control weather conditions around a pool without actually enclosing it. This means a wind-free setting and sun and shade precisely where you want it. Sometimes it can be done with partial overhangs from cabanas and fencings, while at other times it is done by encircling the pool with protective landscaping, fencing fiberglass, and other materials, leaving the top completely open. Ask your builder or architect about the advantages of having a sheltered pool on your site. There may be none. Or if he advises sheltering it, you can put up a minimum amount now and add on later.

Landscaping

The term landscaping covers a multitude of decorative possibilities. The cost is almost entirely up to you. Landscaping need not be done at once. You can spread topsoil and sprinkle it with grass seed, and you can add your shrubs and plantings year by year, although the overall plan should be consistent. For those who like to garden, the results can be stunning. Near the pool, eating area, or on the perimeter near the fence, landscaped shrubs can add visual appeal and serve as protective screening. The patterns can be formal, symmetrical, or have a natural look. You can use rocks, boulders, trees, and shrubs, create waterfalls or lily ponds, and go low key or dramatic. The landscaping plan should reflect your family's life-style and tastes.

Landscaping can create the impression of space where there is none or make your poolside seem more cozy and intimate than the terrain actually is. It can disguise problem areas and mistakes, provided you know how to do it. Look for balance, height, and depth proportions. Will tall trees and high landscaping be in proportion with a low ranch-style home? Will you obscure a lovely view of the mountains or city skyline?

Plan carefully, seek professional advice, and consult design plans. With a solid notion of what will look best for your pool site, you can be creative and innovative but avoid a cluttered, haphazard effect.

Special Problems As mentioned earlier, one of the big disadvantages to an above-ground pool is that it causes landscaping problems. This is particularly true when the pool is placed in the middle of a flat lawn. You could try placing the pool close to the house and then build decks around it. If the decks all tie into the house properly, you can give the effect of an in-ground pool for a small percentage of the cost. Another popular alternative is to place the pool on a slight slope. This requires some excavation of the slope to ensure that the pool itself is on a level spot. But if one side of the pool is close to the ground, new options are created, for example, decks and hedges for shelter and comfort.

A wooded site, handled carefully during excavation, can be left in its natural state for additional privacy and a wilderness effect. Photo courtesy of National Swimming Pool Institute

Accessory Structures

There is a wide variety of accessory structures you can add around your pool. These include cabanas, saunas, dressing rooms, gazebos, or any other enclosed or semienclosed structure. If you are working with a strict budget, this is the area where costs can easily be trimmed.

As a do-it-yourselfer, you will find that there are kits on the market for prefabricated saunas and other bathhouse structures. No carpentry, plumbing, or electric work is necessary. Many manufacturers even ship the prefabricated buildings partially assembled. You can get a portable redwood sauna about the size of a closet, ready to be plugged into an ordinary 110-volt outlet. This type is insulated for interior use only. For exterior use, saunas run slightly larger, about $6 \times 6 \times 7$ feet high, with redwood inside and aluminum outside. You can purchase only the sauna equipment and instructions, and then build your own housing. Dressing rooms and bathhouses are also available in complete kits. Some aluminum models with baked enamel finishes feature two dressing rooms. One can be converted for storage space to accommodate the pool equipment.

In planning an accessory structure, see what is immediately available on your homesite. You may not have to start from scratch. Is there a storage shed that can be turned into a cabana? Part of your garage? A trellis with an outdoor shower could be all you need.

Here are some features which you may incorporate into a bathhouse or use by themselves. You should look for good drainage, privacy, a place to hang clothes and towels, a shower (hot water is not essential), sit-down bench, and perhaps a heater.

All of these facilities are, of course, not necessary, and many can be created separately depending on budget and need. A smart-looking drying rack can stand by itself. A portable dressing room can be nothing but a wood cubby or canvas tent setup. An outdoor shower need not have walls around it, if it is planned well. The variations are almost endless, and so are the prices. You will have to check around to see what you can get or build for your money.

Saunas

More and more American families are making the sauna bath an integral part of their home. Many saunas are located near the swimming pool since sauna bathing requires cold-water dousing as the final step. They are often part of a separate outbuilding or a feature of a cabana adjoining the swimming pool. Discovered by the Finnish people over a thousand years

Patterned wood decking and shed roof make poolside living easy. Photo courtesy of California Redwood Association

A variety of choices for the do-it-yourselfer makes building a dressing room, cabana, or sauna a personalized project. Photos courtesy of California Redwood Association

The change rooms and fencing tie in with the contemporary style of the houses. Note the white birch tree at left—one of the best trees for poolside planting. Photo courtesy of California Redwood Association

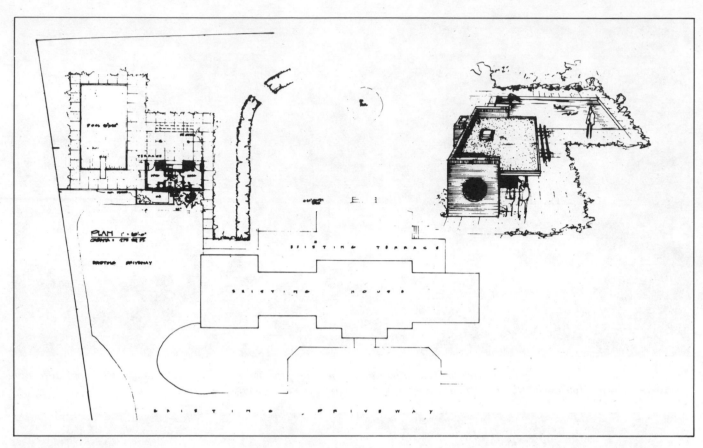

Bathhouses, cabanas, and saunas can be built in a variety of configurations, layouts, and designs. An architect details two different styles of structures and placements for the same pool. Designs courtesy of Robert Crozier & Associates

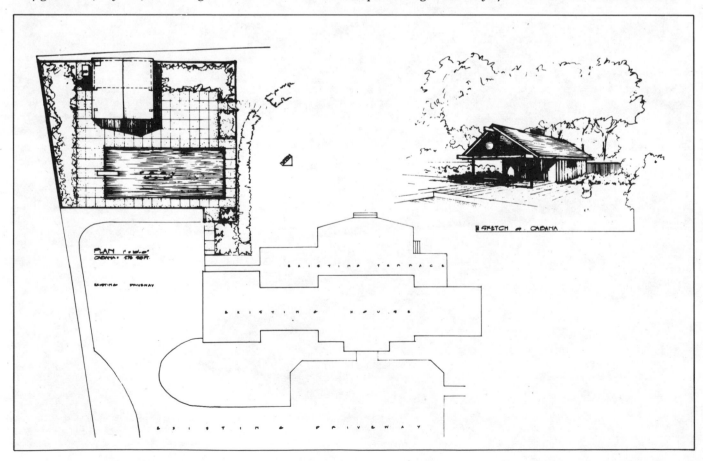

ago, the sauna is a convenient way to shed tension and relax tired muscles.

Many Scandinavian families have relied upon the sauna for generations, considering it almost as essential to their well-being as food or drink. Finnish athletes to this day insist upon having saunas in their Olympic Games quarters.

The traditional Finnish sauna was a small detached building, heated with a wood-stoked furnace piled high with stones to retain and radiate heat. It often took eight or nine hours to reach the desired 175 to 200 degrees Fahrenheit.

Most modern saunas are prefabricated units which can be quickly assembled in a variety of sizes to accommodate from one to four or more persons. Custom-made units also can be built to the buyer's specifications.

A modern sauna can be made ready in fifteen minutes or less and provides fully automatic temperature control. In the American version, humidity is held to 8 percent or less, making the high temperatures comfortable. Some units contain rocks, onto which you pour a few drops of water for a touch of high humidity at the end of the sauna.

Although the Finns use aspen wood, kiln-dried clear all-heart and A-grade redwood is an adequate substitute for the modern-day sauna because of its ability to withstand extreme temperature changes. Redwood acts as an insulator on the walls, ceiling, and floor. It diffuses the heat so the surfaces remain warm, but not hot, to the touch unless they get wet.

Standard packaged saunas on the market range in size from 3'4" × 3'4" to 8' × 12' and have an inside

Am-Finn saunas are prefabricated and prepackaged in four sizes to occupy 24, 40, 64, and 80 square feet of floor space and to accommodate from three to fifteen persons. The units can be assembled and ready for use in a few hours, requiring no need of block wall or studding. Wall and roof panels are of "sandwich" design with poured-in-place polyurethane insulating core. Clear heart redwood is used for the interior walls, floor, and ceiling. The residential application pictured here occupies a former walk-in clothes closet.

height of 6'6". Depending upon size, the units come with one to five benches and will accommodate up to eighteen persons. Custom designs can be ordered prefabricated for fast assembly at the site. Freestanding floor and wall-mounted electric heaters vary in wattage from 5,200 to 15,000, depending upon room size. The UL-listed units are operated by remote controls, or in the case of two smaller models on the market, the heater and controls are built into the door.

Prefabricated saunas consist of insulated panels (designated A through F) and a preassembled door (G). The heat control panel is built into panel F for fast connection to existing power source.

Water Treatment and Filters

Once your pool is completed and filled with water, its care and cleanliness are up to you. Swimming pool water can be deceptive to the untrained eye. It can be sparkling clear while harboring potentially dangerous germs, or it can appear turbid and thoroughly uninviting, yet be safe for swimming. Maintaining water quality, therefore, involves the dual task of keeping it both germ-free and attractively clear.

Swimming pool water quality is maintained by adding the proper amount of disinfectants to kill germs and algae, and by operating an adequate filtration system to remove particles suspended in solution.

Disinfectants

Although you don't need a chemistry degree to maintain disinfectants in the water, you should know something about the chemicals you are using. Pool owners, can handle their own disinfectants, although you may prefer to hire a pool company to maintain the water.

Chemical disinfectants must be added on a regular basis to keep water pure. A disinfectant in the water will attack and kill germs, algae, and other organic matter. As it attacks these organisms, the disinfectant is used up. Therefore, enough disinfectant must be added to kill the bacteria already there, as well as some extra disinfectant to kill new germs. This extra amount is called the swimming pool residual.

For this disinfectant to work at maximum efficiency, the pool's pH must be in balance. A pH is a relative measurement of the alkalinity or acidity of a substance. The pH scale ranges from 0 to 14. A pH of 1 indicates a very strong acid solution. A pH of 13 or 14 indicates a very strong alkaline solution. Your pool water should never be in either of these extremes but balanced between 7.2 and 7.6 on the pH scale. Because 7 on the scale indicates a neutral solution (such as drinking water), your pool water must be just slightly alkaline. You must keep close tabs on your pH level, or you are asking for trouble. If the water becomes too alkaline, your disinfectant becomes very sluggish and will not properly kill germs. If your pH falls below 7 (into the acid region) your disinfectant becomes unstable, and the water will corrode your pipes and other metal parts touching the water. If you have a plaster finish, it may etch the substance.

Test kits are available through every pool dealer. These kits measure both your pH and the amount of disinfectants in water. The kits cost between $10 and $25 and are absolutely necessary for proper water treatment. Without them you are only guessing at the amount of disinfectant in the water. You should have an accurate reading of your pool water and allow a germ count of no higher than zero.

Types of Disinfectants Available

Three basic types of disinfectants are in use today. Chlorine is the most popular, but bromine and iodine are also effective. All three chemicals are members of the halogen family.

Chlorine In its natural state, chlorine is a very dangerous gas. Although it can be used in its gaseous state as a disinfectant, we do not recommend it for home pools. Commercial swimming pools often use gas, but it is maintained in a pressure tank and requires an automatic feeder or chlorinator which regulates the amount fed into the pool.

Liquid chlorine, used in residential pools, is unstable if stored for very long. Because of this instability, manufacturers often add alkali to liquid chlorines. Due to the nature of this mixture, the pH in the swimming pool tends to rise after a while as more and more of the disinfectant with alkali is added. To counter this you must add an alkali-neutralizer such as muriatic acid or sodium bisulfate to the water.

Calcium hypochlorite is a dry form of chlorine that comes either in a granular or tablet form. This chemical has the same problem as the liquid mix in that it tends to raise the pH of the water. Lithium hypochlorite is also a dry stable compound, with less of a tendency to raise the pH of the water, although it certainly will in time. Chlorinated Iso Cyanurate is a dry, stable organic compound that has a longer life and therefore a longer effectiveness in pool water than the other dry compounds. This compound differs greatly from the other inorganic compounds, and the manufacturer's recommendations must be closely followed.

Bromine In its elemental state, bromine is a very heavy liquid with germ-fighting capabilities similar to chlorine. About twice as much bromine by weight is required to maintain the same residual as chlorine. Liquid bromine is a dangerous chemical. If spilled on the body it causes severe burns, and if inhaled it will do damage to the lungs. When this form of bromine is used, mechanical feeding equipment becomes necessary.

Bromine is more active than chlorine in destroying ammonia in the water. Because of this, bromine is effective in pool situations where chlorine is not. This chemical is also subject to less dissipation in sunlight and will produce a more stable residual than chlorine, without the use of a stabilizer. Many people who use this disinfectant also claim that eye irritation is lessened.

Stick bromine is an effective disinfectant that can be handled in much the same manner as dry chlorine compounds. It has the added advantage of not greatly affecting the pH of the water.

Iodine When iodine is used as a pool disinfectant, the pH of the water must be carefully controlled. In its natural state, iodine is a crystal solid. To make it soluble in water, it must be combined with another chemical such as potassium and an activating agent such as hypochlorite.

There are two key benefits to using iodine in pool water: all users agree that there is little or no eye irritation with iodine, and it remains active longer than chlorine. But it is not effective against algae.

Quantities Needed In swimming pools residual chlorine must be maintained at a level between 0.6 to 1.0 parts per million (ppm). This amount of chemical is small in comparison with the total volume of water in a pool but is absolutely essential to maintain purity.

There are a number of factors that can decrease the strength and, therefore, the killing power of your disinfectant. These include:

- The bathing load: as the number of swimmers increases, so does the amount of disinfectant used up.
- Sunshine: the greater the amount of light on your pool's surface, the faster the disinfectant dissipates.
- Airborne grit: particles and bacteria blown into your pool by the wind or on rain droplets cause the disinfectant to work harder and to lose strength.
- pH balance: the higher the pH, the slower the chemical will react against germs; thus, more chemical must be added to maintain the proper residual.
- Total alkalinity: should the total alkalinity drop below the 80 to 100-ppm level, the pH will fluctuate widely and your pool plaster may etch due to high acidity. If the alkalinity is too high, the pH will be maintained at too high a level, and the disinfectant will not be fully effective.

Total alkalinity is the measurement of the total amount of alkaline chemicals in the water. It refers to the degree of resistance to pH change of pool water or its buffering capacity. The proper alkaline level should be between 80 and 100 ppm. As discussed earlier, certain forms of chlorine, if used over a length of time, can affect the total alkalinity of water. Experts say that as a rule of thumb, 1½ pounds of sodium bicarbonate (baking soda) will increase the alkalinity of 10,000 gallons of water by 10 ppm.

If you fill your swimming pool from the tap, chances are you already have a great deal of alkalinity in the water. To lower this water into the proper zone, between 80 and 100 ppm, muriatic acid must be added. The amount of acid needed is referred to as the acid demand.

Bringing Disinfectant to Proper Level A simple test kit is available to let you quickly test and adjust the disinfectant in your pool. If the test indicates you have too little disinfectant in the pool, you must add disinfectant.

You need only a small amount of pool water in your test tube. Add a measured amount of the color-reacting chemical supplied with the kit and compare the water sample's resultant color with a set of standard colors in the kit. The color will tell you the amount of residual. If the test tube color is pale then the amount of residual is low. If the sample is deep, then the amount of residual is high. If the sample matches the color between 0.6 and 1.0, then no chemical need be added.

Superchlorinating Your Pool Swimming pool water contains ammonia and other compounds of nitrogen. Chromides are formed when the chlorine in the water combines with these substances. These chromides cause the eye irritation and chlorine odor often evident around pools. If you smell chlorine around your pool, there probably is not enough residual chlorine in the water. Adding chlorine about three or four times a week during hot weather will probably be sufficient.

To burn out the ammonia and nitrogen compounds in your pool, one of the treatments undertaken every other week should be a superchlorination. You should use about three to four times the regular dosage for this and do it before sunrise or after sundown, when the sun's rays will not dissipate the chlorine.

To decrease chlorine dissipation caused by sunlight, add cyanuric acid to help filter out ultraviolet sun rays to increase the effectiveness of the chlorine. Test kits are available for this, and directions should be followed closely.

Keeping Water Clear

Few, if any, pools built today do not contain a filtration system. The filtration system is the most essential pool accessory. This system is relatively uncomplicated. It usually consists of a pump, a tank with a filtration medium, a hair and lint strainer, surface skimmer, and piping.

Water is drawn into the system by the action of the pump which conducts the water from the pool through the lint strainer, through the filter, and back into the pool as clean water. All equipment used in this system should be of a corrosion-resistant material such as stainless steel, bronze, copper, or plastic.

The cost of this system is almost always contained in the pool package—whether it be an extensive in-ground pool or an above-ground do-it-yourself package.

The filtration system rarely removes germs from the water. Its function is to remove the dirt and other particles that are suspended in the solution which make the water cloudy. The size of the filtration system depends on the volume of water in the pool and the swimming load.

Although there are a variety of filtering systems on the market, the two systems most commonly used on residential pools are the high-rate sand filter and the pressure-diatomaceous earth filter.

Sand Filter The action of the pump in the system builds up pressure and forces the dirty water into the sand. The tiny particles are trapped by the sand and held there. After the system is in operation for a while, the filter medium begins to fill up with dirt from the swimming pool. It must be cleaned before it becomes clogged. Most systems are cleaned through a process called backwashing.

During backwashing, the direction of the water in the filtration system is reversed. This surge of water forces particles away from the sand and washes them out either into a sewage system or a dry well. Once the particles are purged from the filter, it is again ready for use. The system can also be cleaned with a water hose, but this requires considerably more time.

Diatomaceous Earth Filter Often called a D.E. filter, this system uses very fine grain sedimentary rock which is the fossil remains of tiny aquatic plants called diatoms. The tiny fossils are very porous and contain many small passages and channels. Water passes through this material easily, but the openings are so small that particles suspended in water are trapped and held by the media. This substance is so efficient that a few inches of the material will have the same filtering qualities as a few feet of sand.

Backwashing of this filter is accomplished in the same manner as the sand filter.

The size and type of filter you need for your pool depend on the volume of water and swimming load. If your filtration system is too small, it will not adequately clean your pool. If it is too large, operating the system could be very expensive. Seek expert advice before purchasing a system. Your pump and filtering tank must be of the proper ratio to generally keep the pool clean. Water must pass through a filter three times to get the water 95 percent clear. Experts call this a turn. Water that passes through a filter once is clear, but it is then reintroduced into the pool where it is diluted by the turbid water. This process of filtration and dilution continues until the water is relatively clear.

For a typical 20 × 40 foot in-ground pool, one filter is usually enough. The system should filter the water at least once every eight to twelve hours.

Water and Your New Pool

After the new swimming pool has been completed and filled, the pool contractor will normally supervise or advise the new owner on proper treatment and care. Some of the larger contractors will insist that either they or another knowledgeable person service the pool in the beginning as a precaution against errors and to keep the warranty good.

Iron in the Water If, however, you must take over the testing from the beginning, begin before the pool is filled. One of the first and most important tests is for iron in the water. Iron is not a problem in most areas where tap water is used. But if water is used from an underground source, testing for iron is essential.

To test, fill a jar with water and add about ½ ounce liquid chlorine. Agitate the liquid inside the bottle and let it sit for an hour or two. If the water darkens, iron or manganese is present. Once you have determined the presence of iron in your water, contact a knowledgeable person before filling the pool, especially if there is plaster in the pool. If your pool is already filled and you want to get rid of iron, there are two generally accepted methods. You can add chlorine to the pool to precipitate the iron out. Only a small amount of chlorine should be added at a time. When particles form at the bottom of the pool, they should be vacuumed out immediately.

Another method is to "floc" the iron out. First dissolve potassium alum in the water, to form aluminum hydroxide, a gel-like substance which traps iron particles. This substance is then removed from the water through the application of the pool filter system. Usually one pound of potassium alum will clear about 5,000 gallons of water. While this process is taking place, it is advisable to vacuum the particles which have settled on the bottom of the pool. The whole procedure requires about forty-eight hours.

Test for pH Once the pool is filled and you are satisfied that there is no iron in the water, test for pH. There are a variety of test kits available for this.

As mentioned, pool water should be maintained between 7.2 and 7.6 on the pH scale. The chemicals used for testing the pH should always be fresh. If your chemicals are one year old, discard them and purchase a fresh supply.

Fill the test tube with pool water. Add the proper amount of PhenolRed to the water. When pool water is too acid, the water in the test tube turns yellow. When it is too alkaline, it turns red. Comparing the test tube's color with the standard color supplied with your kit indicates the water's pH.

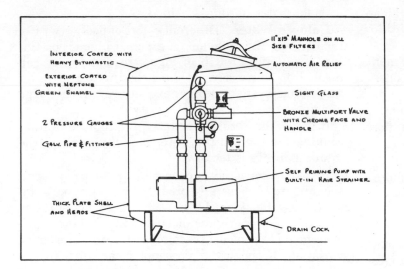

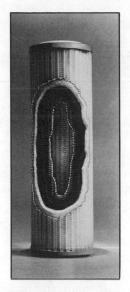

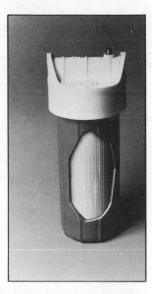

Here is a diagram showing the parts of a residential sand and gravel filter. Photo courtesy of Neptune Filters

The diatomaceous earth filter, or DE, uses a fine grain sedimentary rock which is the fossilized remains of tiny aquatic plants, called diatons, to filter the pool's water. Photos courtesy of Johns-Manville

Once you determine how much your water differs from the recommended 7.2 to 7.6 range, add enough chemicals to bring it in line. Because chlorine can affect the pH of your water, you should make this test when the chlorine residual is low.

Do not use your finger as a stopper while making this test. The human body contains acid, and the residue on your skin could give you a false reading. Use the stopper supplied in the kit.

There are a variety of chemicals available to use in balancing pH. The usual chemicals are soda ash to raise the pH (related to baking soda and one of the most inexpensive) and muriatic acid to lower the pH. Commercial strength muriatic acid is about 30 percent hydrochloric acid. This acid is dangerous and should be handled and used carefully. You should not add more than one pint of muriatic acid to every 5,000 gallons of water at a time. Let it sit and retest the next day. No one should swim in the pool after acid has been added.

Water Problems

Algae A number of water conditions can arise from time to time due to the weather or the bathing load, but the most common problem is algae.

Through proper conditioning of water, algae problems can be avoided. Although fairly simple to prevent, algae is often difficult to remove. What complicates the problem of algae once it gets a foothold is that there are at least 46 fresh-water varieties.

Planktonic clean-water algae floats on the surface. Other types attach themselves to side walls or bottoms and are tough to remove. Fresh-water algae can be green, blue-green, red, brown, or black. It can cause unpleasant tastes and odors, turbidity, slippery spots, and increased chlorine demand.

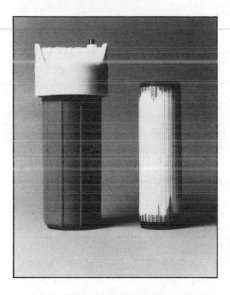

Sunlight, pH, temperature, bacteria, and mineral content all affect the presence and growth rate of algae. Algae can be present in the source water used to fill the pool or introduced by wind-borne particles, rainwater, or fallen leaves.

The best preventive measure is to keep the pool's pH balanced and the chlorine at the proper level. An occasional superchlorination is also effective in preventing algae.

If algae does get a start in your pool, check the pH to make sure it is in the proper range. Then check your total alkalinity and adjust it to the 80 to 100 ppm range. Superchlorinate your pool with the filter off for about twenty-four hours. Turn your filter on, brush sidewalls, and vacuum dead algae.

When selecting an algaecide for your pool, keep in mind that:

- It should be effective against all strains of algae found in swimming pools, especially the hard-to-kill black algae.
- It should be independent of chlorine treatment and should not interfere with chlorine as a disinfectant.
- It should remain effective between treatments.
- It should be of low toxicity so it does not affect swimmers.
- It should not be absorbed by the filter.
- It should precipitate out of the water or combine with the chemicals routinely used in the pool.
- It should be easy and economical to use.

Hard Water Hard water is another major swimming pool problem. Hard water that causes problems in the washing machine or bathtub can also damage swimming pools. Hard water contains excessive amounts of dissolved minerals including magnesium, manganese, calcium, sodium, and iron. While several of these substances will show up when you test for total alkalinity, others will not. Calcium and magnesium sulfates, chlorides, and nitrates and several other compounds constitute permanently hard water.

Your swimming pool can suffer from pool ring, similar to the telltale bathtub ring. Hardness can affect pH. If the pH becomes too high, turbid or cloudy water will result, and possibly pool scale formation and skin and eye irritation.

You test for hardness at poolside with one of the test kits available or the soap test. The soap test is performed by adding some household soap solution, drop by drop, to a small amount of pool water in a test tube. After a few drops are added, the tube is shaken. The end point is reached when a thin layer of lather remains on the surface of the solution for five minutes. For the inexperienced pool operator, it is probably best to purchase a test kit and add the recommended chemicals for water hardness reduction.

Colored Water Different colors of pool water can indicate specific problems. A green or blue-green tint can reveal the growth of algae; reddish water can mean iron is present; a blackish tint to the water might mean that manganese is present in large amounts, although this is a rarity.

If the water is turbid or hazy, the total alkalinity could be too high. If the water is milky, perhaps the total alkalinity is too low.

If your water is not a deep blue or the color corresponding to that usually produced by your pool's colored side walls, it may be that the water is not properly filtered and properly disinfected with a balanced pH. You should take measures immediately to correct such variation. If the water does not clear up with the adjustments suggested, call in your pool contractor or pool dealer to treat the problem before it gets out of hand.

Staining If water is not properly maintained, staining can result. This is usually most obvious when iron is present. If not taken care of, a reddish stain will result. Should black algae get a foothold, a black stain will appear.

There are other ways that a pool can become stained. A swimmer may drop an object that will rust or corrode into the pool. A daily maintenance program should include an inspection of the pool bottom and removal of any objects inadvertently dropped in.

Scale Scale is the buildup of substances such as calcium. This results when the pH of the pool is allowed to become too high. The buildup will first be detected on heating coils but can also be seen on tiles and concrete. If at all possible avoid this problem. Small amounts can be removed with sandpaper, but when a substantial buildup occurs, professional help and power tools will be needed to remove it.

Pool Maintenance and Repairs

Proper swimming pool maintenance is important to you for two primary reasons: it will afford you years of trouble-free use and help you protect a very substantial investment. Unlike a new car, a swimming pool does not depreciate in value after only a few years. But like a car, it needs regular care and maintenance and occasional repairs to keep it at peak performance.

One of the most common questions asked by people shopping for a swimming pool is: "How long will it last?" If you ask contractors or swimming pool dealers and receive only vague answers, chances are they are not trying to skirt the question. They don't know. It is entirely up to you. A quality in-ground pool can last indefinitely if cared for properly.

Contractors who have been in the business many years report that in-ground pools they built in the 1930s are as good today as when they were first filled. Others, of similar quality, have fallen into decay. What makes the difference is how well the pool has been maintained.

To keep your pool at maximum operating efficiency year in and year out, you must supply regular care, seasonal care, maintenance, and occasional repairs.

Maintenance

According to the NSPI and other authorities, you should create a seven-point checklist of regular-care items and then see that it is carried out.

Manually Skim Pool's Surface Pools collect a great deal of debris and junk just by being outside, not to mention what swimmers drop into pools. Although your pool probably has an automatic skimmer, some hand skimming is usually required.

There are many good hand skimmers on the market. A hand skimmer may be included as part of the package, but if you must shop for one, get one with a 12 to 16 foot handle. Although all this length is not necessary for surface skimming, you may have to fish out material which has sunk to the bottom.

The best time for skimming is either in the morning or in the evening, when there are no bathers in the water. The proper way to skim is to begin at extended length and pull toward you. Continue to pull and to lift up and then remove from the pool and empty.

Brush Down Walls and Tile If you keep on top of it, you can hold stains and growths down to a minimum through a regular brushing program. The best brush for this is either a stainless-steel brush or a unit with nylon bristles.

First, brush walls around pool perimeter and then brush the floor from shallow to deep end. This prevents dirt buildup in corners and mixes the settled dirt with the water, so it can be removed via the filtration system.

Black algae leave stains that are particularly hard to remove from pools. Sometimes the growth can be scrubbed, and when residual chlorine attacks it, it may die. If this does not work and the stain becomes very unsightly, you may have to drain the pool and apply muriatic acid.

Unless your pool is quite small, draining it is a serious matter and should be done only after consultation with or under the supervision of your contractor or pool dealer. Applying acid to the wall will remove the stain, but it may etch the surface, which can shorten the life of your pool. If your walls are painted, you can always touch them up after the stain is removed.

Clean Skimmer Basket There is no special equipment required to clean the skimmer basket and hair-lint strainer. To do this, remove the skimmer basket and the pump's lint strainer and take out all debris that has collected. Then replace both.

Do this during the swimming season about once a day. In the spring and autumn when there is a heavy fall from trees and shrubs, it should be done more often. Failure to keep baskets clean will result in reduced circulation, introduction of air into the system, and possible loss of the circulating pump prime.

Vacuum Pool Bottom Pools should be vacuumed at least once or twice a week. New pools usually come equipped with a vacuum system that plugs into a special suction fitting built into the pool which gets its suction from the pump. There is an automatic vacuum system available. Your local pool dealer can help select one suitable for your setup.

Clean the Pool Filter Because there are various types of filters on the market, it is difficult to give advice on general servicing. As a rule of thumb, all types of filters (slow sand, pressure or vacuum diatomite, and high-capacity sand) should be serviced at least once a week. Diatomite types should probably be serviced more often.

At a certain point, the filter will collect a sufficient amount of dirt so that pressure will rise within it, and the recirculating flow will decrease substantially. This is when the filter must be backwashed. Although most filters operate in a similar fashion, manufacturers' instructions should be consulted.

Treat the Pool Chemically Use only your test

kit. No other special equipment is needed to treat your pool. Things to keep in mind while testing the water daily include: the level of residual disinfectant, algaecides, proper pH, and total alkalinity balance.

Hose Pool Deck Area It is rather useless to maintain water purity if the area around the pool collects debris, dirt, and bacteria.

The immediate area around the pool should be hosed down daily. This will help greatly in keeping the swimming pool itself clean. The changing room, bathroom, or other facilities immediately around the pool should also be maintained in sanitary condition to stop the spread of bacteria.

Seasonal Pool Care

To ensure a long life for your pool, a proper program of seasonal care is as important as your regular program during the swimming season. If you live in a warm climate where you can use your pool most of the year, some of the following information applies. If you live in a cold climate, you must follow certain guidelines, listed here, for winterizing your pool. Properly preparing your pool for winter will not only save your pool wear and tear, but it will make spring opening a lot easier.

For Cold Winters Equipment: Just as your car's radiator will burst if you do not use antifreeze, your pool's equipment will be damaged if water is allowed to freeze in the pipes, filtration system, heater, and pump. If you are not going to drain your pool, have antifreeze added to the pipes, after having the air in them blown out to create a vacuum. Plug the pipes once antifreeze is added. Both addition and removal of antifreeze should be done by a serviceman.

Emptying the pool: There is considerable debate about emptying pools in the winter. Consult your pool contractor on this. Should damage occur over the winter because you emptied your pool, it may not be covered in the warranty. Check your warranty.

Pull all the plugs on your system, and let the water drain out. Consult the instructions given with your pool. Also, be sure to drain all other waterlines which are above the frost line.

If you do empty your pool, you will not have slime buildup or waterline stains to contend with in the spring. On the other hand, an empty pool is subject to

Seasonal pool care may include emptying your pool (after consulting with your builder). This is the perfect time to get in there and scrub it out thoroughly, watching especially for stubborn stains, as from black algae. Photo courtesy of Johns-Manville

After emptying the pool for seasonal care procedure, it's a good idea to check up on any damage your pool walls or tile line have incurred during the year. Photo courtesy of Johns-Manville

During the swimming season, it's a good idea to clean the skimmer basket daily. By cleaning grass and other debris from the basket, good water circulation is ensured. Photo courtesy of Johns-Manville

Vacuuming the pool once or twice a week during the swimming season should be part of a pool owner's maintenance program. Photo courtesy of Johns-Manville

ground pressure which could cause your pool to float. This is particularly true of vinyl-lined pools. Sudden changes in air temperature can also cause your pool surface to crack. Frost is another enemy of empty pools. It works around the perimeter of pools and can cause serious cracks.

If your pool remains full over the winter, you should test the water occasionally and adjust chemicals as needed. This bit of care will go a long way toward cutting your work in the spring.

Dropping your pool's water level a few feet is probably the worst compromise of all. You still have slime and stain buildup to contend with in the spring, and your pool is still liable to suffer from frost conditions and rapid temperature change.

Storage: To get maximum use of your poolside equipment and accessories, take away those that are removable and store in a dry area until spring.

Pool covers: Pools collect debris over the winter. Falling leaves and other objects get blown into the pool, and rotting vegetation can cause difficult stains. If at all possible, put a cover over your swimming pool. Without one you will have to skim the pool regularly.

There are three basic types of pool covers: summer, winter, and year-round. The lightweight polyethylene covers for summer offer overnight protection but lack durability. Winter covers can be made from vinyl-polyethylene-constructed fabric which may become stiff and weaken in lower temperatures and will sink if

torn. Coated polyethylene and polypropylene will not stiffen, and since they are lighter than water, they will float if torn. Year-round covers are made of porous poly materials and because they do not puddle (collect water from rain or snow), the need to siphon off water is eliminated. These materials sustain weight up to 200 pounds.

For Warmer Winters If you are in a warm climate, it is better to leave your equipment in operation to hold algae buildup to a minimum. As in a cold climate, however, you should test your pool's water and adjust chemicals as needed.

For Spring How much work will be involved in opening your pool for the swimming season will depend on how well you prepared your pool the previous autumn and what you did over the winter.

If you did nothing, your pool will probably be filled with algae, vegetation, and stains. In this instance, it might be best to drain the pool for proper cleaning. Consult your contractor before draining.

If you can drain your pool in the spring rather than in the autumn, it will be much easier to clean and check. The main problem at this time of year is that the ground around your pool is usually sodden with water. The hydrostatic pressure may, therefore, be at its greatest. If, however, you have a good relief valve in your pool, the danger of float will be lessened.

Whether you drain your pool or not, the following steps should be observed before you start the swimming season:

- Pump and filter: Check your filter pump for damage from freezing. Check and clean the baskets and the "O" ring. If there are any breaks or ragged edges in the "O" ring, it should be discarded and replaced with a new one.

The filtration system should now be cleaned and lubricated according to manufacturer's specifications. Again, look at "O" rings and replace worn ones. The filter material should be carefully examined. Is it cemented solid or channeled? Although filter material can last for years, a damaged filter cuts severely into filtration efficiency. Filtration material is inexpensive to replace.

If you have a diatomite filter, open up the system and hand-scrub the filter with a detergent, spray clean, and replace.

- Pipes and lines: Check out all lines. If you used winterizing plugs, remove them. Look for freeze damage on all lines and make sure they are in good condition. If not, call in a service repairman.
- Heater and other equipment: Check your pool heater tubes for scale buildup and look at the wiring for breaks or shredded insulators. A simple cleaning in the spring can prevent a burnout later.

Check out all your other equipment, such as your pool light. If the interior is flooded with water or corroded because of moisture, remove it from your pool and have a service company repair it.

Bring all your accessories and equipment out of storage and go over them with a cleaning agent before reinstalling.

- Pool and water: If you have tile around the pool, clean it. Give the walls and floor of your pool a good brushing (drained or full), prime the pump following your manual's instructions, and start recirculating the system. If your pump is noisy once you begin operation, this might indicate worn bearings. Consult an expert on this repair.

It is wise to purchase a new water-testing kit each year. Reagents from last year tend to lose their potency and can cause problems later on in the season when you need an accurate reading of the water.

Repairs and Troubleshooting

Unless you are experienced with swimming pool equipment, it is probably best to leave major repairs to a reliable swimming pool service. But here are a few tips on what to look for before you call the repairman.

Pumps You may occasionally run into problems with your swimming pool pump. It may be clogged with debris or leak. If you suspect pump trouble or motor trouble, never run your pump dry under any circumstances. All pumps are water-lubricated, and if the pump runs dry, the motor will quickly be damaged.

In most cases, however, the problem is not in the pump itself but rather the pump motor. Before you call the repairman, break the seals and remove the pump motor. These seals are designed to prevent water from getting into the mechanism. If you locate the trouble yourself and are able to fix it, you will need to purchase new seals before putting the pump back together.

For a clogging problem, look at the suction line, impeller, or the strainer basket. The suction line may be clogged with debris. Most pump impellers can also become clogged with hair and other debris over a long period of time. The remedy for this is to disassemble the pump housing after removing the motor and motor shaft with impeller, and clean it. Look at the strainer basket; it may simply be full and require emptying and cleaning. Again, remember to replace all broken seals with new ones.

For water leakage, look at the pump shaft. If the leak is there, it is a sure sign that the seals need to be replaced.

If you cannot locate the problem yourself or are unable to fix it once you have discovered the problem, call your pool serviceman.

Filtration System If you suspect malfunction in your filtration system because it takes too long to recycle clear water back into your pool, check first for trapped air. Open the manual air release until all air is expended. During the swimming season, you should do this once a week as part of regular swimming pool care.

If there is an automatic air release on your filtration system, check to see if this is clogged and therefore malfunctioning. In this case you must look at your manual for instructions on disassembling the mechanism. Once disassembled, clean it thoroughly.

If after cleaning either the manual or automatic air release you are still getting air in the line, check to see if you have a leak in the suction line. If you do, call your serviceman.

When your diatomite filter is not doing the job, the filter may not be properly cleaning during the backwashing cycle. To correct this, remove the filter and clean it. If it still is not functioning properly, try soaking it in a solution of muriatic acid (1 to 5) for about half an hour.

Poor filtration in the sand filter might be due to channeling within the filtration material. This allows the water through without being properly cleaned. In this instance, replace at least 1 foot of sand.

Pool Safety

Owning a swimming pool is both a pleasure and a responsibility. Responsibility for the safety of the persons using the pool rests with the owners. A few common sense precautions taken as part of the swimming program of the whole family can lighten the burden.

Establish sensible pool rules at the very start and make sure they are enforced until they become second nature in the pool-use routine. It may be wise to write out your rules and post them where anyone using the pool can see them.

Along with your rules, also list where you keep your safety equipment such as a first aid kit, ring buoy, and the telephone numbers of your family doctor, hospital, police, and rescue unit. Precious life-saving seconds can thus be saved in an emergency. Although your family should be well versed in rescue situation procedures long before they are needed, a simple diagram of how they are done could be crucial to visitors.

In-Pool Rules

A few swimming and diving rules should include: precisely what games are safe fun (water volleyball, floating checkers, and others) and what constitutes dangerous horseplay. No one should ever use the pool alone, no matter how expert a swimmer he or she may be. Anyone who cannot swim should be carefully supervised and given lessons by a qualified person. Inexperienced swimmers should stay out of the deep end of the pool.

One person at a time should use the diving board or slide. Absolutely no horseplay is allowed here. Playing around or under the board or slide should not be permitted when they are in use.

Diving boards and slides should not be installed in residential pools which are not built to accommodate them. Check with your pool builder. Make sure your board cannot be adjusted to provide too much spring for the amount of water depth available to catch the diver safely before he or she hits the bottom. Keep the nonslip surface of the board in good repair. Jump boards and water slides require the same attention and care as do diving boards and should be firmly anchored.

Children gravitate to a pool like bees to honey, but never let them play in or around the pool without close and continuous adult supervision. Rest periods keep children from getting overtired or overexcited. Everyone should rest after eating to prevent cramping and ensure proper digestion.

Besides maintaining safety rules which cost nothing but the time invested in practicing them, safety equipment should also be purchased.

For younger children, a fence, wall, or building structure enclosing the pool, at least 4 feet high which they cannot open or climb over, is advisable. This barrier should have a self-closing lock and permanent locking hardware above toddlers' reach. Inflatable toys which support children in the water are also deflatable. Fences within the pool area to enclose toddlers are found helpful by some families.

A minimum amount of money must be spent on a good first aid kit and a lightweight but strong pole with blunt ends at least 12 feet long, or a ring buoy with a long throwing rope firmly attached. This constitutes basic lifesaving equipment.

Safety equipment can also include inexpensive items such as deep-water markers—ropes and buoys—or higher priced items such as resuscitators. Special hand grabs, ladders, or steps can offer safety features for those families which feel they will be used to good advantage. Pool covers are a good investment in safety for those families which will not be using their pool during certain months of the year.

There are all sorts of pool alarms now on the market. When no one should be in the pool area, an alarm can be connected so that upon entrance to the area the alarm goes off. Another type uses a weight; anyone falling or entering into the water sets off the alarm.

Poolside Safety

Swimming rules and safety equipment are important, but don't underestimate poolside behavior. Decks around the pool should be kept clear of debris. Cigarettes or cigars should be carefully put out in ash trays at least a foot or two off the ground. Make sure all glasses and dishes used at poolside are nonbreakable.

Electrical equipment used for the pool should conform to local regulations or the latest National Electrical Code requirements. Never allow electrical appliances near the pool that have not been protected by a ground fault circuit interrupter.

Suntan oils are fine for the poolside, but should be washed off before anyone enters the pool itself. These oils are hard on the pool's filtration system.

Proper water treatment and filters keep the pool in a healthy condition for swimming. Storing chemicals and cleaning agents out of reach of children or adults who do not know the proper procedures for use is a very wise precaution. A locked, dry area (not the filter room), inaccessible to children and nonexpert adults, is a good storage spot.

Usually an ordinary homeowner's insurance policy will cover a swimming pool without any additional charge. You should notify your insurance agent, however, that you have added a swimming pool on your land. He or she might suggest some additional coverage.

There should be periodic safety and maintenance checks to all pool appliances and equipment. If you need help, locate a local NSPI builder or service company which can provide these services.

SAVING A DROWNING VICTIM THROUGH MOUTH-TO-MOUTH RESPIRATION

Individuals who die as a result of a water accident usually die from the lack of air, not from water in the lungs or stomach.

A drowning victim may be either be active or passive. Unless unconscious, the person will usually struggle to remain on the surface to get air. These efforts may result in the person swallowing a varying amount of water. To make matters worse, water swallowed and in the lungs may cause a person to regurgitate this water and food, blocking the air passages and thus interfering with the rescue effort.

Here are a few simple procedures to follow for the mouth-to-mouth method of artificial respiration from The American National Red Cross:

(1) Tilt the head back so the chin is pointed upward. Pull or push the jaw into a jutting-out position. These maneuvers should relieve obstruction of the airway by moving the base of the tongue away from the back of the throat.

(2) Open your mouth wide and place it tightly over the victim's mouth. At the same time pinch the victim's nostrils shut. Or close the victim's mouth and place your mouth over the nose. Blow into the victim's mouth or nose. (Air can be blown through the victim's teeth even though they may be clenched.)

(3) Remove your mouth, turn your head to the side, and listen for the return of air, which indicates air exchange. Repeat the blowing effort. For adults, blow vigorously at the rate of about 12 breaths per minute. For a child, take relatively shallow breaths appropriate for the child's size at the rate of about 20 per minute.

(4) If you are not getting air exchange, recheck the head and jaw position. If you still do not get air exchange, quickly turn the victim on his side and administer several sharp blows between shoulder blades.

You should time your efforts to coincide with victim's first attempt to breathe for himself.

If vomiting occurs, quickly turn the victim on the side, wipe out the mouth, and then reposition.

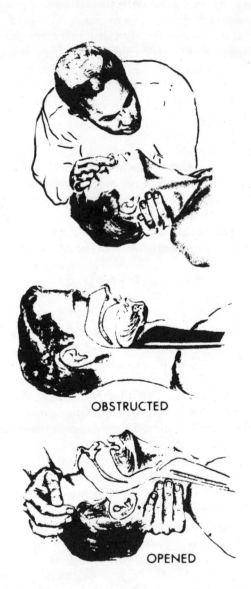

OBSTRUCTED

OPENED

Glossary

Algaecide A chemical used to kill algae.

Alkaline The property of a chemical which allows it to neutralize acid. If the swimming pool pH reads above 7, the water is alkaline.

Alkalinity The amount of hydroxide ions present in a solution.

Alum One of several aluminum compounds used in swimming pools to form a gelatinous floc on sand filters or to coagulate and precipitate suspended particles in water.

Ammonia A chemical compound of hydrogen and nitrogen which combines with free chlorine in pools to form chloramines. This condition in swimming pool water causes burning eyes, skin irritations, and the odor usually associated with chlorine.

Available Chlorine Chlorine, either free or combined, which is active against bacteria and germs in pool water.

Backfilling When hole excavated for pool is greater than the pool structure, it must be backfilled with earth. One should use caution in backfilling; do not allow heavy machinery too close to pool walls or heavy rocks to fall against walls.

Backwash The process of cleaning the swimming pool filter by reversing the water flow.

Bacteria Microorganisms present in all water supplies including swimming pools. Chlorine and other chemicals are used to keep these microorganisms under control.

Bacteriacide Any of a number of chemicals used to kill bacteria.

Breakpoint The point at which a rising concentration of chlorine in swimming pools kills germs and bacteria by oxidizing organic matter. Once all matter is oxidized, the amount of chlorine remaining is free or uncombined.

Bromide A chemical compound containing bromine, a halogen. Sodium or potassium bromide in solution will produce free bromine if chlorine is added to the pool.

Calcification Buildup of calcium carbonate on swimming pool walls and equipment. This stems from precipitation of calcium from hard water.

Calcium Hypochlorite A chemical compound of chlorine and calcium used as a bacteriacide in swimming pools. It comes in white granular or tablet form and releases 70 percent of its weight as available chlorine.

Chlorine A heavy, green, and highly poisonous gas compressed into liquid form and stored in heavy steel tanks. It is used in swimming pools as a bacteriacide and algaecide. In most residential pools, chlorine is rarely used in its gaseous state.

Chlorine Demand The amount of chlorine necessary to oxidize all organic material present in pool water at a given moment or over a period of time.

Chlorine Residual The amount of chlorine remaining in pool water after the chlorine demand has been satisfied at a given moment. This chlorine is available to oxidize other bacteria in water.

Clarity The transparency of pool water.

Coagulant A chemical compound, usually alum, used in pools for the purpose of gathering and precipitating suspended matter.

Combined Chlorine Chlorine which is available as a bacteriacide in water but which is combined with another substance, usually ammonia. Combined chlorine is usually less effective against bacteria.

Conditioned Water Generally refers to initial conditioning of the water with cyanuric acid.

Copper Sulfate An algacide declining in popularity today because of its toxicity and incompatibility with some other compounds found in pools.

Corrosion A reaction on the surface of metal parts of swimming pools, causing deterioration.

Cyanuric Acid A compound which is used for initial pool conditioning.

Filter A device for straining suspended particles from pool water.

Filter Aid Usually refers to a powderlike substance such as diatomaceous earth or volcanic ash used to coat a septum-type filter. Can also be used to refer to alum as an aid to sand filtration.

Filter Cycle or Filter Run The time of filter operation between backwash procedures.

Filter Media Fine-grain material that entraps suspended materials as they pass through the material.

Filter Rate The rate of water flow through a filter during the filtering cycle, expressed in gallons per minute per square foot of effective filter area.

Filter Septum Part of a filter on which diatomaceous earth or similar filter media is deposited.

Flatplate Collector The most common and often-used collector in a solar system; the most visible portion of a solar system appearing on the roof or in the yard.

Floating Swimming pools can have their floors pushed up if enough water pressure is allowed to gather around it. This condition, called floating, is virtually impossible if the pool contains water. When pools are emptied, however, damage can occur.

Floc A gelatinous substance resulting from the mixture of a flocculent, such as alum, with alkaline compounds.

Flocculent A compound, usually some type of alum, used with sand-type filters to form a thin layer of gelatinous substance on the top of the sand. Aids in trapping fine suspended particles which might pass through the floc.

Hardness (in water) Refers to the quantity of dissolved minerals, such as calcium and magnesium compounds.

Heat Pump A combination heating and cooling device. In the winter it extracts heat from air as cold as 20 degrees, and in the summer it works in reverse to become an air conditioner.

Hydrostatic Relief Valve A valve installed in the main drain of the swimming pool, sometimes in other areas as well. When pool is full, the valve is closed; when pool is empty, it is opened to allow ground water to flow into pool. This prevents the pool from floating, which happens if ground water pressure builds up.

Iodine A chemical compound containing iodine. Potassium or sodium iodide, when used with a suitable oxidizing agent such as chlorine, will release iodine in pool water.

Lint Strainer A device mounted in the pump influent line to catch lint and other debris.

Make-up Water Fresh water used to fill or refill a swimming pool.

Multifamily Pool Swimming pool mutually owned by several families. One family can use a pool without footing total expense.

Muriatic Acid A solution of diluted hydrochloric acid.

Oxalic Acid An organic acid, usually a solid, white granular substance. Used to dissolve iron rust stains on pool walls and floors or to clean iron rust from filter septa.

Parts per Million (ppm) In swimming pools, the parts of a chemical or mineral per million parts of water by weight.

pH A measure of the degree of acid or alkaline quantities a solution possesses. Below 7, the solution is acid. Above 7 it is alkaline.

Phenol-Red A dye which is yellow at a pH of 6.8 and turns a progressively deeper red color as the pH increases to 8.4. This is the most commonly used test reagent for pH in swimming pools.

Potassium Alum Sometimes used as flocculent in sand filter operation.

Scale A crusty deposit of mineral salts on heating coils and pool surfaces.

Skimmer A piece of equipment other than an overflow trough for continuous removal of surface water and floating debris from a swimming pool. Usually the water is removed to the filtration system.

Skimmer Weir The part of the skimmer which adjusts to small changes in water level to assure a continuous flow of water to the skimmer.

Soda Ash Sodium carbonate is used in swimming pools to raise the pH and increase total alkalinity. It is also used with alum in sand-type filters to produce floc. When chlorine gas is used as a disinfectant, this chemical is used to neutralize hydrochloric acid.

Sodium Bisulfate A powder which produces an acid solution when dissolved in water. Compound is used to lower pH in water and is considerably safer to handle than hydrochloric acid.

Sodium Hypochlorite A liquid that contains between 12 and 15 percent available chlorine. This compound is commonly used in swimming pools to produce chlorine. It produces hypochlorous acid when added to pools.

Sodium Thiosulfate A chemical compound used to remove all chlorine from a test sample to avoid false pH test readings or false bacteria test results.

Solar Heating System A device for capturing the sun's rays, and a system to transfer that heat to a storage area where it is held until needed.

Superchlorination An extra treatment of pool water with three to four times the regular amount of chlorine to burn out nitrogen compounds when bacteria, algae, or ammonia are extremely built up.

Swimming Load The number of persons in the pool area at any given time.

Total Alkalinity Actual amount of alkali salts present in swimming pool water.

Turbidity Degree to which pool water is visually obscured by suspended particles.

Turnover Rate The number of times a quantity of water, which is equal to the total capacity of water in the swimming pool, passes through the filters in a given period. This is usually expressed in turnovers per day.

Underdrain The distribution system at the bottom of a sand filter to collect the filtered water during a filter run and to distribute the backwash water during backwash.

Underwater Light A lighting fixture designed to illuminate a pool from beneath the water surface. It can be wet-niche, located in the pool water, or dry-niche, located in the pool wall, and serviced from outside the pool.

Vacuum Cleaner One of several types of suction devices used to collect dirt from the bottom of the pool. These units work in a variety of ways. Some force collected dirt to the filter, others to a waste drain or into a porous container.

Volcanic Ash A fine powder similar to diatomite but lighter in weight. It is used as a filter media or filter aid in diatomite filters.

Index